I0284609

Ogun

The Ultimate Guide to an Orisha and Loa of Yoruba, Santería, and Haitian Voodoo

© Copyright 2023 - All rights reserved.

The content contained within this book may not be reproduced, duplicated, or transmitted without direct written permission from the author or the publisher.

Under no circumstances will any blame or legal responsibility be held against the publisher, or author, for any damages, reparation, or monetary loss due to the information contained within this book, either directly or indirectly.

Legal Notice:

This book is copyright protected. It is only for personal use. You cannot amend, distribute, sell, use, quote or paraphrase any part, or the content within this book, without the consent of the author or publisher.

Disclaimer Notice:

Please note the information contained within this document is for educational and entertainment purposes only. All effort has been executed to present accurate, up-to-date, reliable, and complete information. No warranties of any kind are declared or implied. Readers acknowledge that the author is not engaging in the rendering of legal, financial, medical, or professional advice. The content within this book has been derived from various sources. Please consult a licensed professional before attempting any techniques outlined in this book.

By reading this document, the reader agrees that under no circumstances is the author responsible for any losses, direct or indirect, that are incurred as a result of the use of the information contained within this document, including, but not limited to, errors, omissions, or inaccuracies.

Your Free Gift
(only available for a limited time)

Thanks for getting this book! If you want to learn more about various spirituality topics, then join Mari Silva's community and get a free guided meditation MP3 for awakening your third eye. This guided meditation mp3 is designed to open and strengthen ones third eye so you can experience a higher state of consciousness. Simply visit the link below the image to get started.

https://spiritualityspot.com/meditation

Table of Contents

INTRODUCTION 1
CHAPTER 1: WHO IS OGUN? 3
CHAPTER 2: OGUN AS A SAINT 13
CHAPTER 3: ARE YOU A CHILD OF OGUN? 22
CHAPTER 4: OGUN IN MYTHS AND LEGENDS 31
CHAPTER 5: WHAT OGUN TEACHES HIS FOLLOWERS 42
CHAPTER 6: OGUN'S SYMBOLS AND OFFERINGS 55
CHAPTER 7: MAKING A SACRED ALTAR 67
CHAPTER 8: USEFUL RITUALS AND SPELLS 76
CHAPTER 9: OGUN'S FESTIVALS AND HOLY DAYS 85
CHAPTER 10: DAILY RITUALS TO CELEBRATE OGUN 92
EXTRA: GLOSSARY OF TERMS 99
CONCLUSION 101
HERE'S ANOTHER BOOK BY MARI SILVA THAT YOU MIGHT LIKE 103
YOUR FREE GIFT (ONLY AVAILABLE FOR A LIMITED TIME) 104
REFERENCES 105

Introduction

Have you ever wondered what secrets lay within the ancient religion of Yoruba? Do you want to uncover the mysteries of Ogun, the God of Iron? In this book, you'll explore the secrets of Ogun's divine power and learn how to incorporate Ogun's teachings into your everyday life.

For centuries, the Yoruba people of West Africa have celebrated Ogun, a deity revered for his life-giving and transformative energy. He is cited as the ancestor of warriors, hunters, artisans, and those who brought culture and technologies (like ironworking) to the area. This incredible technology transformed the region's culture by easing laborious tasks with tools made out of iron. The region was strengthened through cultural exchanges, such as ivory carving, metalworking, and furniture making.

In honor of Ogun's transformative energy, devotees still celebrate him at the annual Ogun festival in Nigeria. During the festivities, reverential monks invite blessings from the god and offer magical objects in exchange for blessings. They are hopeful that these rituals will bring great fertility to their crops and ensure protection against any untoward situations in their lives and community. This book will explore various aspects of Ogun's worship, including his symbols and offerings, rituals and spells, holy days and festivals, and daily rituals to celebrate him.

Ogun is an amazing figure who has been worshipped worldwide since ancient times. He is known for his strength and power, and those qualities are evident in his presence across the continents. Many cultures have embraced him as a god of protection or a patron of metalwork, such as that performed by blacksmiths or warriors. Through this incredible reach, Ogun has shared his power with people from all walks of life, allowing them to embrace his awesome strength daily!

This book explores the depths of Ogun's power, and readers will learn how to invite his divine gifts into their lives. It will also uncover the secrets of his symbols and offerings, delve into rituals and spells, and discover how to celebrate his festivals and holy days. At the same time, it explores why Ogun is still relevant today and what he can teach followers about the power of strength and courage.

Ogun, the fourth king of Ife and the Yoruba people, was a warrior and protector god who brought multiple blessings to the kingdom. His worship is still alive amongst many who strive to honor him with small festivals, music, and offerings. The secrets of Ogun's worship, which hew to ancient traditions, are carefully guarded. However, it's possible to pay homage to this fascinating deity and learn more about his past through this book. Readers will gain invaluable insight into the power and mystery of Ogun and how to make the most of his gifts. Happy exploring!

Chapter 1: Who Is Ogun?

Yoruba and Haitian Voodoo are two spiritual traditions with powerful histories passed down through the generations over centuries. It's incredible to think about how long these two practices have existed. The concept of a shared cultural identity between African people is inspiring, as it shows that regardless of where people come from, everyone can still be connected by their roots. While the two practices may seem different on the surface, they have many core values, symbols, and practices in common. This is an example of the strong spirit of unity that transcends time and place.

Yoruba and Haitian voodoo have a powerful history within many communities.
Calvin Hennick, for WBUR Boston, CC BY 3.0 <https://creativecommons.org/licenses/by/3.0>, via Wikimedia Commons
https://commons.wikimedia.org/wiki/File:Haitian_vodou_altar_to_Petwo,_Rada,_and_Gede_spirits;_November_5,_2010..jpg

Ogun, an illustrious figure in the Yoruba religion and Haitian Voodoo faith, is among the most revered figures in these two sacred traditions. Ogun is worshipped as a warrior god and guardian of iron. He is seen as a protector who can fight off evil forces. On either side of the Atlantic, believers seek his strength and guidance for protection in times of need. Whether found on the African continent or the Caribbean island of Haiti, it's easy to see why Ogun is such a significant part of both civilizations' spiritual life!

This chapter will explore the concept and significance of Ogun in the Yoruba and Haitian Voodoo religions. It will discuss the characteristics, spellings, rituals, offerings, and associations in each tradition, as well as their differences and similarities. It will also show how Ogun is viewed in both cultures and how he is connected to his other identities. By the end of this chapter, you should better understand Ogun's importance and relevance in the Yoruba and Haitian Voodoo religious beliefs.

Overview of the Yoruba and Haitian Voodoo Religions

The Yoruba and Haitian Voodoo religions have a long and fascinating past, stretching back hundreds and hundreds of years. Both religions are tied to the African diaspora, tracing their origins back to West Africa. They each offer insight into the spiritual practices of the people who created them and have impacted many other cultures worldwide. While their customs, beliefs, and traditions may differ significantly, their common ancestry still connects these faiths profoundly. It's incredible to think that they remain so influential despite having such distant points of origin!

Originating from African cultures, these faith systems were brought to the Caribbean by enslaved African people during the diaspora. Both are unique religions steeped in rituals and practices used for divination, healing, and prayer for protection. All of these practices involve elements of nature, such as magical charms, ancestral spirits, and sacred objects. The Yoruba spread to other parts of Africa and the Americas, while Haitian Voodoo mixed with Catholicism over time. These religions emphasize living harmoniously with one's environment, which is very relevant in the modern world. By understanding the foundation and tenets of both Yoruba and Haitian Voodoo, you can learn more about each other's cultures and healing practices and how you can better honor this shared planet.

Ogun across Yoruba and Haitian Voodoo Religions

Ogun is a prominent god in Yoruba and Haitian Voodoo religions and African Diaspora spiritual systems. He is known as the Orisha of metal, strength, war, and protection, among other things. In the Yoruba religion, he is one of the most powerful spirits, charged with leading other spirits in times of crisis. In Haitian Voodoo, Ogun's special focus is to bring luck to his devotees along their journey in life. The rhythmic chants used to honor him emphasize his importance and power. Across these two religions and even beyond Africa, people who revere Ogun honor him in different ways. Some pray while others perform rituals such as dancing accompanied by drums or banging tools relating to his affinity with metalwork.

Ogun in the Yoruba Religion

Ogun holds a lot of significance for those who follow the Yoruba faith. His importance lies not only in providing protection and guidance, but his biggest impact is on the culture itself. Ogun teaches humility, respect, justice, courage, and industry. He is credited with enforcing laws and creating avenues for artistic expression through song, dance, poetry, and sculpture. As one of the most powerful gods of Yoruba mythology, Ogun inspires generations with his strength, devotion, and love for the Yoruba people.

Ogun is considered the god of ironwork and war and is celebrated by one of the biggest religious festivals in Nigeria, a weeklong event during which people come from all over to pay homage to Ogun. Worshipers offer him yams and other foods as he is known for providing abundance when prayers for success are answered. Ogun appeals to all classes, embodying hard labor and courage as he pushes through obstacles and finds solutions to any challenge.

A. Characteristics

Ogun is an Orisha warrior god with incredible symbolic potential. He is associated with the metal-smithing trade and represents the strength and power of iron. His presence is strongly felt whenever people are busy constructing things from metal or otherwise manipulating its form.

He's seen as a beloved protector who watches over warring parties to help bring about peace and a kind-hearted figure who provides advice and assistance to mortals in times of need.

Ogun possesses unique characteristics that give him unquestionable authority and immense wisdom, making him highly respected among his followers. Regardless of the task at hand, when Ogun's guidance is sought after, he never fails to bring about positive results for those who call upon him, making himself irreplaceable in Yoruba religious practices.

B. Symbolism

Symbolically, Ogun is associated with strength, justice, and being a protector of the people. He is often depicted as a warrior, representing his willingness to physically fight for what he believes in. Additionally, it is said that Ogun created tools and imbued traditional medicines such as herbs or protective charms with his powers and which are used for healing and protection. In other words, Ogun's symbolism represents not only the battle but also accomplishment and construction.

The machete is another significant symbol associated with Ogun, as it represents the physical strength of warriors and is also a tool used to cut through any obstacles that may be standing in the way. Other symbols include fire, swords, and horses, all meant to represent Ogun's readiness to fight for what is right. The colors red, black, and white symbolize Ogun as they represent the element fire, which manifests his power.

C. Rituals

The Yoruba religion has many unique practices, including the ritualistic worship of Ogun. Derived from their ancient African folklore, this deity stands for strength, courage, and determination. It holds a vital place as a spirit guide who helps lost souls find their way back to safety. Although his presence can be overwhelming at times when it comes to combat, he ultimately serves to protect those in need.

His rituals are often incorporated into ceremonies like birth rites and fertility celebrations as a symbol of progress and security in the community. Some of the rituals and festivals dedicated to Ogun involve offerings of food, drink, and in some cases, sacrifices. It's interesting to consider how traditional practices such as these have been able to endure throughout time and remain influential in modern society today!

D. Offerings

Ogun is seen as a powerful ally with the ability to protect and give guidance throughout life's struggles. His offerings are believed to be highly beneficial for those looking to improve their physical and spiritual health. It's not uncommon for offerings of food, specially prepared meals, or even metal tools or statues of Ogun himself to be placed at his altars to honor his presence.

Offering tribute to the influential Ogun of Yoruba faiths is a meaningful way to express gratitude and respect for his many blessings. Tributes demonstrate appreciation and maintain a positive relationship with this powerful figure. Whether it's in the form of daily prayers, artwork, jewelry, or other offerings, being mindful of worshiping Ogun through tributes can profoundly impact your life. It's one small step that can reap big rewards.

E. Association with Other Gods

Ogun is an openly revered god in the Yoruba religion, along with Obatala and Ile. He is a symbol of strength and courage, offering protection to those who call upon him. Ogun is also associated with ironworking and new beginnings, so he holds a special place in marriages and initiations into adulthood. People who follow the Yoruba faith will often leave offerings for him at crossroads to mend any grievances that may have arisen. He brings life-sustaining elements like rain, the wind, and fire which are necessary for everyday life. In short, Ogun is an important part of the Yoruba religion and is highly regarded as a protector and foundation of well-being amongst followers of the faith.

Ogun in the Haitian Voodoo Religion

Ogun is an influential lwa in the Haitian Voodoo religion. He's frequently depicted as a soldier dressed in either red or white, holding a machete and smoking a cigar. As in the Yoruba religion, Ogun is the lwa of metal, iron, and weapons, making him the protector of people who labor for their living using such tools. He's also deeply associated with technology since he guards and controls the machines humans use to perform physical tasks, making him an essential deity in contemporary Haitian culture, where many inhabitants integrate technology into their lives.

Ogun, the powerful son of Yemaya, is great to have on your side. His passion for justice and his fierce wrath towards evil have earned him a place in the pantheon of many African tribes. Yet Ogun also shows a sweet reverence towards those who pay respect to him by honoring and understanding his power. If an offering is made with proper respect and admiration, he will offer protection and blessing to whoever requests it. His presence brings strength, courage, and true healing to those within his realm.

A. Origin of the Loa

Ogun is an essential figure within Haitian Voodoo and plays a big role as the Warrior God or Lord of Iron. He is considered to be a guardian of travelers and a protector from danger. On top of this, he symbolizes strength, courage, assertiveness, creativity, and fertility, the attributes that many venerate in their daily lives. Ogun was first introduced to Haitians with the arrival of African slaves in the 18th century. Before then, worship of the Loa was unknown.

The slaves adopted Afro-Caribbean spiritual traditions such as Vodou, integrating them into their belief systems while keeping ancient secrets alive throughout generations. This explains why Ogun remains so important to Haitian people today. He has roots deep within the country's history and continues to promote resilience among its citizens.

B. Role in Haitian Voodoo

Ogun is an essential figure in the Haitian Voodoo religion, a major African-Caribbean faith. Ogun, sometimes referred to as the "Warrior God," represents a powerful spirit associated with control and protection. Those who worship Ogun will often pray for his assistance during difficult times of struggle and unrest. He is seen as the guardian of justice and protector of all living things. His skill at protecting from enemies and misfortune is renowned throughout the religion and by anyone engaging in Voodoo practices or seeking guidance on a spiritual journey.

Worshipers are encouraged to always show their utmost respect for Ogun, offering various types of offerings, such as sacrificial animals that represent peace and prosperity. Beyond this, Ogun has become increasingly popular even in non-Voodoo circles. Travelers, adventurers, business professionals, students, athletes, and others also seek out his guidance and protection when embarking on life-changing events or projects.

C. Characteristics

Ogun is seen as fierce, powerful, and unyielding. He's a necessary figure for times when his followers feel overwhelmed and must draw on power from within themselves. He is known to be passionate about justice and economic success and can provide both protection and guidance. He is often imagined as dressed in red with a machete in hand. He is associated with fire, steam, or smoke rising from the fire used in ancestral ceremonies. He provides strength and integrity to those who venerate him. Worshipping Ogun enables Haitians to feel empowered regardless of their circumstances, something that has been particularly valuable throughout Haiti's long history of oppression and upheaval.

D. Connections to Other Loas

Holding a place of prominence in the Haitian voodoo religion, Ogun is often referred to as the god of iron and war, but his impact on religion goes far beyond that, representing technology and progress. Ogun has many connections to other Loas in this religion, like Baron Samedi and Damballah. For instance, like Baron Samedi, Ogun connects with leadership and guidance. Like Damballah, who represents communication and emotions of connection with oneself during difficult times, Ogun is a loa who takes on the role of protector of those who are at their most vulnerable. All these shared connections make him an important part of the Haitian Voodoo religion's tradition and practice.

E. Offerings

People honor Ogun by having rituals set around iron implements and giving offerings such as four-sided nails or blades. It is said that if respected, Ogun has the power to make unimaginable changes in an individual's life. As a representation of strength, protection, justice, and growth, offerings are made to Ogun on specific days in the hopes of receiving his goodwill and blessings. Offerings such as tobacco are also given to keep Ogun appeased. It is believed that those who have called on Ogun's blessing can receive immense power over their destinies if they follow their dedication through. Ogun is truly a unique symbol of power and resilience from the Haitian Voodoo religion.

Comparing Yoruba and Haitian Voodoo

Yoruba and Haitian Voodoo have many similarities and differences, making them both unique and fascinating. Yoruba is distinct in its roots, which go back to traditional African beliefs, while Haitian Voodoo has kept its iconic voodoo dolls around for centuries-long. Both practices put faith in deities, sacrificial offerings through ritual ceremonies, consulting with spirits or gods to receive advice or blessings, and use talismans for protection.

Nigerian practitioners embrace a more communal approach to the practice, usually gathering together in groups during ceremony time, and are mostly centered on family lineage, whereas practitioners of Haitian Voodoo seek out solitary rituals, take their solo path outside the prescribed ceremony setting, and ask help from powerful Loa spirits. All in all, Yoruba and Haitian Voodoo remain fundamentally different yet similar in many ways.

In Yoruba tradition, Ogun is also called Ogou, Ògún Lákáayé, or Ogúm depending on the individual worshipper's affiliations and preferred dialect. His power over human existence through creativity and production has meant that even today, adherents will seek out his assistance when working with iron or undertaking political actions. Whether pacifistic or fierce, Ogun offers guidance to those dedicated to the transmission of knowledge across time and space.

However, Ogun is known as a Loa (spirit) in Haitian Voodoo. His presence holds a similar importance in Haiti's religious traditions as he is an intermediary between the spirit world and humanity. Ogun is a champion of justice, a creator of order, and a defender of those who have been wronged. He is often seen with an axe in hand, a symbol of his ability to clear the way for spiritual communication and connection.

Ogun's dual roles in Yoruba and Haitian Voodoo offer a fascinating insight into the differences between these two religions. While both traditions honor him as a spirit of strength and protection, how he is venerated differs. In Yoruba, Ogun is seen as an Orisha, who is worshiped and celebrated through rituals and sacrifices, whereas in Haitian Voodoo, he is seen as a Loa, or one who an individual can summon for direct communication and help. This illustrates the central difference between these two religions. Yoruba worships and appeases Orishas and other powerful spirits with ritual ceremonies. Haitian Voodoo places a greater emphasis on the autonomy of individuals, meaning that people are free to choose what they do. With the help of devotees, individuals can gain a deeper comprehension of a Loa's power and use it to their advantage.

A. Commonalities

Yoruba and Haitian Voodoo are fascinating forms of spirituality with incredible similarities. Although they may have originated in other parts of the world, both share common African roots. Both practice similar concepts, such as ancestor veneration, encouraging resilience from believers, and teaching them how to live purposeful lives. Even though traditional creeds differ in practices and foundational beliefs, the power structure and relationship between humans and gods are shared. Thus, the spirit of universality within both religions continues to unite diverse peoples who practice different faiths in respectful discourse and understanding.

B. Differences

The topics of Haitian Voodoo and Yoruba are a great way to learn about the distinctions between different cultures. Both faiths have been practiced for centuries throughout the same geographical region, yet distinct differences make each one unique. While both traditions rely heavily on spirit attachments, Yoruba focuses more on appeasing these spirits with ritual ceremonies, while Haitian Voodoo places a greater emphasis on the autonomy of individuals with activities like possessing worshippers and controlling their behavior. Haitian Voodoo also allows for the possibility of even creating new gods. All in all, studying the disparities between Yoruba and Haitian Voodoo opens one's eyes to how two divergent cultures can take fundamentally similar approaches yet still yield two drastically different results.

Ogun's Other Identities

Ogun is associated with metalworking, war, and other titles such as the God of Blacksmiths and Warrior Deity. While Ogun is famously known for his warrior spirit, he's also revered as a god of creativity, technology, and growth, offering divine inspiration to those who work with their hands to make things in life. His metalworking abilities allowed him to shape symbols of power, weapons that could both protect and harm if necessary. He has historically been seen as the patron saint of protection in times of war while providing guidance and strength during peaceful times.

Ogun, regarded as the patron of ironworkers, is one of the African religions' most powerful and widely-revered deities. Ogun's domain extends across all aspects of life, playing a part in procreation, marriage, birth, and death rituals. For example, traditionally, couples about to get married invoke his name while asking for a happy marriage. His influence is also extended beyond the realm of human activity. Ogun is often asked to protect fields from damage by animals or inclement weather. As an orisha (deity), Ogun plays an integral role in the local culture. His presence permeates many Nigerian traditions, both collectively and individually.

In Yoruba and Haitian Voodoo, Ogun is revered as a strong, powerful, and reliable spirit. He offers protection, guidance, justice, and strength in times of hardship. His roles as a deity of creativity, metalworking, and warfare make him one of the most popular Orishas/Loa in African religions. Despite his different names, titles, and roles, Ogun remains a powerful and influential spirit for people of both religions. He embodies strength, courage, and resilience in difficult times. Followers of Ogun are compelled to use his courage and strength in times of uncertainty, knowing that he will never abandon them regardless of what happens in their lives!

Chapter 2: Ogun as a Saint

Santeria, also known as La Regla Lucumi, is an Afro-Caribbean religion that blends elements of Yoruba and Haitian Vodou traditions with Roman Catholicism. It is especially popular in Cuba, but there are also a large number of followers in the United States as well. While Santeria honors both ancestral gods and those of African diaspora religions, the primary belief system is based on the veneration of Catholic saints and Jesus Christ himself.

Santeria is a religion that blends Vodou traditions with Catholicism.
Nheyob, CC BY-SA 4.0 <https://creativecommons.org/licenses/by-sa/4.0>, via Wikimedia Commons https://commons.wikimedia.org/wiki/File:Saint_Luke_Catholic_Church_(Danville,_Ohio)_-_stained_glass,_Saints_Teresa_of_Avila,_Clare_of_Assisi,_Monica,_and_the_Immaculate_Conception.JPG

The ritual practices associated with these saints give devotees a way to connect their spiritual beliefs with their everyday realities. Different levels of complex initiation rites must be completed before someone can become a part of the religion, though many devotees tell stories of receiving guidance through visions or dreams. All in all, Santeria encourages its followers to live harmonious lives with other cultures and religious systems.

This chapter will explore the role of Ogun in Santeria and how he is syncretized with various saints. It also discusses his protective capabilities and the offerings made to him. By the end of this chapter, you'll have a deeper understanding of how Ogun is venerated in Santeria. You'll also have a better appreciation for the spiritual power of Ogun and understand how his influence can be used to protect both individuals and their communities.

Introduction to Santeria

Santeria is a vibrant and colorful religious tradition that originates from the Caribbean islands. It is a polytheistic religion rooted in West African spiritual traditions, particularly its core beliefs and rituals. Santeria has grown in popularity since it arrived in the U.S., especially due to its eclectic syncretism, which melds African spiritual elements with other world religions such as Christianity and Indigenous American faiths. Santeria recognizes various deities called Orishas, who reflect forces of nature and represent moral values and ethical principles to inspire believers on their journey through life. Practitioners of this vibrant faith seek to create harmony between their visible world and unseen forces while gaining strength, power, courage, and knowledge through each interaction.

Santeria Differs from Yoruba and Haitian Voodoo

Santeria is an intriguing religion where ancient influences meet modern life. It is rooted in the beliefs of the indigenous people of Nigeria and Benin but has been recognized as distinct from both Yoruba and Haitian Voodoo. The primary difference lies in their approaches to magical practices. For example, Santeria seeks to not only present offerings to gods to have one's life changed but also seeks advice from oracular divination, whereas Yoruba and Haitian Voodoo practices focus more on the use of talismans and supernatural powers such as shape-shifters or zombies to respond directly to individual needs. Although it takes elements from all three religious traditions, Santeria is unique in its elements and meanings. Those practicing it believe nothing can happen until the ancestral gods are consulted. It is a process steeped in altruism rather than self-interest, emphasizing responsibility toward community harmony more than personal gain.

Ogun in Santeria

Ogun is a powerful god in the Santeria religion and is seen as a kind and protective deity who gives guidance to passionate individuals who ask for direction. He represents power, strength, and courage while embodying traits like intimacy, fervor, and enthusiasm. He is also known as the deity of war, ironworks, creativity, and hunting. Ogun is often associated with tools used by blacksmiths, such as anvils, hammers, and axes. This makes him one of the most significant deities to pray to for success if you are looking to start your own business or seek luck in any entrepreneurial endeavor.

The Role of Ogun in Santeria

Ogun is Santeria's African Orisha spirit of iron, fire, and war. He is an incredibly powerful Orisha who helps his followers better themselves to gain strength and courage. Ogun teaches that not all journeys have a single path and that he will bring you the power and insight needed to face any challenge, regardless of the difficulty. His signature color is red, and things like tools, weapons, and military equipment represent him as these are the things most associated with his domain. Ogun bestows upon his followers' great courage to deal with misfortune in life and heal their minds and hearts of sadness or sorrow so they can move forward in life, overcoming all obstacles. One thing followers of Ogun must remember is that power isn't just given but must be taken. He will mentor you on the journey with courage while you face the fear of taking action!

The Attributes of Ogun

In Santeria, Ogun is commonly referenced as the "father of all Orishas." He's known for being a warrior spirit and, as you know, is represented by iron and other metals. Ogun is the patron of technology, politics, jobs, and justice. His attributes include intelligence and knowledge, strength, inventiveness, and creativity. These traits symbolize how he can bring prosperity. Worshippers often offer him iron tools so that he can help them with their endeavors. Ogun's colors are green, black, and red, representing his strong connections to the Earth and protection from negative energy. He's also known for his passion and loyalty to those who serve him faithfully. All in all, Ogun is an incredibly important figure in Santeria and should not be overlooked when studying its belief system.

How to Invoke Ogun in Santeria

Santeria is a diverse religion, and many people have been learning its traditions for centuries. Ogun is one of the deities most commonly venerated in this belief system. If you are interested in some ritual practices to invoke Ogun, begin by investing in items that represent Ogun, such as tools or weapons of iron or a red candle. Ensure that you create an altar devoted to him and lay out your goods on it before lighting those candles and presenting offerings like fruit or other foods. As you do, keep petitioning the deity and explain what it is that you need help with, whether it's money, family matters, or education. When ready, close off the prayer with offerings of thanks and slowly finish off the ritual by blowing out each candle with a few words of gratitude directed towards Ogun for hearing your prayer.

Ogun's Syncretism with Saints

Ogun, the powerful Yoruba deity of Iron and War, is one of the most beloved figures in African diasporic religions worldwide. Ogun is celebrated among diverse cultures, which honor him for his multifaceted roles, from work and industry to protection and justice. Interestingly, Ogun has been syncretized with various saints in some folk religious cultures, connecting this powerful West African spirit to Roman Catholic figures like St. George and St. Jerome. By doing so, practitioners can connect with both religious legacies in unique ways and emphasize the shared values of strength, courage, tenacity, and nobility believed to be common between Ogun and such venerated saints. This syncretism highlights how connected everyone is on a spiritual level across time as well as space.

A. Saint Paul

The syncretism between the pre-colonial deity Ogun and St. Paul is interesting. Ogun was widely worshipped across West Africa as a spirit of iron and war, while Saint Paul is widely known today as an early Christian scholar and missionary. This syncretic link between the two faiths provides an opportunity to bridge traditional African religions and Christianity meaningfully. What's more, examining this history of religious mixing can even open up choices for Africans today on how they may pursue conformity (or not) with incumbent views on faith. From the outset, it appears that both beliefs can coexist peaceably in addition to fueling each other's growth – which makes for interesting reading!

B. John the Baptist

Ogun, an important deity worshipped in West Africa, holds a special place in the religious beliefs of Yoruba-speaking peoples. His ties to Christianity are especially noteworthy since he has been syncretized with John the Baptist, who enjoys particular significance in Christian scripture. This represents a blending between two belief systems and speaks volumes about the welcoming and tolerant values of the people of West Africa, who embrace many faiths and create open spaces where all cultures and religions can mix harmoniously. The connection between Ogun and John the Baptist is also interesting from a historical perspective, as it gives you a glimpse into the spiritual changes that have occurred over time.

C. Saint Jacob

Ogun is often syncretized with Saint Jacob in many parts of the world. This unique and fascinating phenomenon mirrors aspects of syncretism found in different belief systems throughout history. Ogun is known for being a formidable fighter, a great predictor of success, and a provider of strength for his followers. The character traits Ogun and Saint Jacob share include compassion, determination, and undying commitment to those they serve. It's no surprise then that so many cultures have found similarities between these two figures, illustrating how traditions around the globe are connected despite the geographical distance.

D. Saint Barbara

Ogun is widely regarded as a saint-like figure in the Yoruba religion. Still, it turns out that his syncretism reaches further than simply being Yoruban. Ogun's source of adoration has been linked to Saint Barbara in both Catholic and Orthodox Christian traditions. A strong connection between the two exists because they are so similar. Both are considered guardians who protect against political strife and other forms of chaos while also watching over crossroads, travel, and justice. The syncretism of Ogun with Saint Barbara appears to be less a combination of figures and more of a recognition of each other's virtues. Celebrating them together is just one way West Africans recognize their connectedness with the rest of the world!

E. Saint Peter

The Catholic Saint Peter is yet another example of syncretism with Ogun. It was believed that Ogun's power and strength could be called on through prayer to Saint Peter, showing how the two stories were interwoven. This is a powerful example of syncretism, blending two seemingly disparate entities and finding a culture, tradition, and power in their unity. Syncretism formed much of the basis for religious traditions for African Americans during the times of slavery - and carried forward even after emancipation; Ogun-Saint Peter is just one of many examples that continue to exist today.

By looking at these synergies, you can learn more about African cultures and the religious beliefs that have been shaped in the diaspora. Syncretism has enabled people of faith to build a bridge between disparate belief systems, creating a link between the divine and mortal world as well as creating a powerful way to express values and honor ancestral figures. Through the syncretism of Ogun with various saints, you better understand how West African spiritual traditions have evolved and why certain deities have become so important to people living in today's world.

Ogun as a Protective Force

In Santeria, he is considered a powerful protective force, a warrior, and a crusader, ready to leap into action to safeguard his people. Worshipping Ogun enables Santeria followers to feel protected within their community. It is believed that Ogun can provide strength when confronted with physical or spiritual obstacles. He also promises security against evil spirits and vigilante justice against any harm that may come to his devotees. Even in difficult times, having faith in Ogun ensures that his followers will not wander unprotected through the world. If you show respect to him, he will reward you with his protection, so it's crucial to honor him however you can.

A. Protection from Evil Spirits and Negative Energy

Thought of as a protective force against any dark forces that seek to harm, Ogun is honored by many practitioners of Santeria, who look to him for protection from evil spirits, negative energy, and generational trauma. He is seen as an extremely powerful weapon to be wielded against the darkness, a shield that will ward away anything with evil intentions. When you call on Ogun's strength and courage, you can feel empowered knowing you have a powerful ally behind you.

B. Uplifting Those in Need

In the Santeria tradition, the African god Ogun is viewed as a powerful force of protection and creation. Ogun is also considered a deity of war in the pantheon of Yoruban gods, but in Santeria, he is seen as more than just that. He is a deity who protects those in need, encourages creativity and changes through innovative thinking, and guards against anything threatening safety or well-being. Those who call on him for help often experience greater clarity in their lives and find the strength to take bold steps forward on their paths. In emphasizing love, peace, and compassion for all living things, Ogun serves as an uplifting force in the lives of those he helps.

C. Physical Protection

Ogun is an immensely influential Santerian figure. He is a powerful warrior, protector of the family, community, and home, and a defender of justice and retribution against oppressors; because of these strong associations with protection, many Santerians will call on him to offer physical safety from harm and maliciousness. Ogun offers a benevolent strength that ensures harmony and balance between the human realm and divine forces. There is something comforting about knowing that you have a powerful figure watching out for you when no one else can protect you. With his help, your well-being can be better secured and maintained.

D. Protection from Harmful Intentions

In Santeria, Ogun is a spiritual force of protection and defense. He guards people against harmful intentions and provides divine assistance to ensure that one is safe from danger. He is believed to be an immensely powerful deity, equipped with supernatural strength, and can overpower any enemy attempting to enter his domain. Ogun is also seen as a symbol of justice and retribution. In some traditions, he represents the fight for power or dominance over injustice, which makes him an effective source of protection for those in need. Through his strong presence, he brings about aid in difficult times and offers safety by deflecting harm away from those under his watchful eye, making him an invaluable asset in Santeria's pursuit of safe havens against dark forces.

E. Protection of the Home

Santeria is a faith practiced by millions of people, and at its center are powerful spirits called orishas. Ogun has long been associated with protection, especially when it comes to guarding homes. Ogun is considered a strong defender who stands ready to ward off evil forces should they ever attempt to cause harm to the inhabitants of the house. He helps not only to protect those within the house but also serves to purify the home and those who inhabit them. Ogun devotees give thanks to this spirit for his watchful presence and pray that his power will always work together with their energy and efforts to provide total safety and security in every home regarded as sacred by Santeria.

Ogun and His Offerings

A much-revered god in the practice of Santeria, Ogun is a powerful spirit and the orisha of war, labor, justice, and iron tools. He has many different facets to his identity, including a warrior spirit who fights for justice as well as a protector of riches and material wealth. Devotees to Ogun give offerings to show respect and appreciation, ranging from cigars or rum to coins or knives, depending on the individual looking for divine aid. People seeking fortune in their work may offer shiny coins, while someone looking for courage may present the orisha with a blade. No matter what the offering, Ogun is honored, usually with fire, and these offerings will be faithfully received.

A. Ebo for Ogun

Santeria is a powerful African-diasporic faith tradition with a strong connection to nature, as seen in the veneration of the Orisha Ogun. Ebo for Ogun honors and reinforces this connection by providing offerings of fruit and vegetables, along with items made from iron and other natural materials. The offering is a way for followers to give back to nature and revere Ogun, the most significant Santerian Orisha. Through these offerings, worshippers can honor his power to shape the physical world while affirming future success and peace. Furthermore, these practices carry symbolic meaning, which opens spiritual connections between humankind and the spirit or divine forces influencing everyday life.

B. Sacrifices to Ogun

The offering of sacrifices to Ogun is considered a form of honoring and offering respect. These sacrifices may include goats, roosters, yams, or other produce native to the region. In many cases, it is believed that sacrificing one's possessions pays greater homage than sacrificing an animal because the personal bond between practitioner and offer is stronger. Regardless of what a Santeria adherent chooses to offer as a sacrifice to Ogun, it should be conducted with love and respect for this generous spirit who so willingly gives his presence within rituals honoring him.

C. Offerings and Appeasement to Ogun

In Santeria, Ogun requires offerings and appeasement to grant his followers protection and abundance. Offerings for Ogun typically involve metals such as iron or copper, even gunpowder. Other sacrificial items, including food, alcohol, cigars, or smoke, may also be used to appease him if desired. If Ogun is invited into a ceremony, he will command attention. It is said that when he speaks, no other voice can compete! It is clear how his presence alone generates immense respect within the Santeria tradition.

Ogun has such great influence in Santeria, and he has many different aspects to his identity, often invoked by followers seeking protection, prosperity, courage, and justice. Offerings made to Ogun can include food, cigars, rum, coins, knives, or animal sacrifices, depending on what the devotee seeks from the spirit. When appeasing Ogun, it is necessary to do so with love and respect for the orisha to grant one's wishes. Ogun can also be syncretized with various saints, such as Saint Paul, John the Baptist, and Saint Jacob.

Each saint brings unique characteristics that make them a suitable companion for Ogun, such as Paul's strength and courage or John the Baptist's devotion and piety. Through these practices, Santeria adherents honor Ogun in a way that is meaningful to their faith and seek divine guidance from a spirit that will always be loyal. Ultimately, what one offers to Ogun is up to individual interpretation and depends on the devotee's desired outcome. Ogun is a powerful spirit who will always answer those who call upon him with love, honor, and respect.

Chapter 3: Are You a Child of Ogun?

African spirituality experts posit that every person has two Orishas or spiritual parents. To epitomize this belief, one of the two is always considered the head of their relationship. In other words, it is thought that your life is not just determined by a single force but rather by a team effort on behalf of your spiritual parents. This double representation gives you the understanding that your life is in no way predetermined and instead is equipped with all the support needed to make the decisions that await you. It is an amazingly empowering concept and further exemplifies the beauty of African spiritual practices and beliefs.

This chapter will explore this concept in more depth and discuss how to identify the Orishas that are your divine "parents" and which one is the head of the relationship. To do so, a simple quiz has been added, which will help you to answer the question posed in the title of this chapter. This quiz lets you check whether your preferences, lifestyle, or personality traits can be associated with Ogun. By doing so, you'll closely examine Ogun's personality traits and characteristics.

Introduction to Divine Parentage

African spirituality is characterized by rich traditions and beliefs that are often steeped in elements of divine parentage. This concept relates to the belief that a higher being created the universe, served as its commander, and is essentially its parent. African cultures understand this power from many perspectives, with names such as Olodumare in the Yoruba culture, Ngai among the Kikuyu people, and Qamata among the Xhosa people. Beliefs about divine parentage generally tie into broader principles of belonging, servitude, order, and respect for synergy across all living beings in their environment and ancestries. Worship around divine parentage is part of celebrating African identity, integrity, and a sense of responsibility. It reminds Africans of their connectedness to something larger than themselves as they strive to be stewards in honoring resiliency through spirit.

Identifying Your "Parent" Orisha

Identifying your "parent," Orisha, is an amazing and important journey. It goes far beyond any test results as it requires knowledge, intent, and respect for the process. In traditional Yoruba religion, every person has a "parent," Orisha, who is their spiritual guardian and offers guidance on their life's journey. Knowing your parent Orisha can open up a world of potential to understanding yourself spiritually. This helps you answer who you are meant to be, what kind of work you should pursue, and the goals best suited to finding happiness. Do some research, speak with elders in the Yoruba tradition, and take time to quieten your mind. With persistence, you can tap into extraordinary levels of insight and clarity that will shape your decisions as you move through life.

The Quiz

Ogun is a powerful Orisha in the Yoruba pantheon and is considered the god of iron and fire. He is associated with strength, power, action, and innovation. Think about the following questions to determine if Ogun is your divine parent:

Do you like a challenge?

Ask yourself if you prefer to take on tasks that require hard work, dedication, and skill. Do you enjoy the feeling of accomplishment after a difficult task is completed?

Are you resilient in the face of adversity?

The path of life often presents many obstacles, but do you approach them with determination and a positive attitude? Are you willing to pick yourself up after a setback and try again?

Do you enjoy taking risks?

Do you often make bold moves to reach your goals? Do you like pushing yourself out of your comfort zone to see what's possible?

Do you prefer to take the lead?

In any situation, do you like to take charge and direct the flow of things? Do you often prefer to be the one making decisions and leading others? Do you have an innate ability to inspire those around you to achieve greatness?

Do you tackle obstacles head-on?

Facing problems can be intimidating, but do you choose to confront them directly? Do you think the best way to overcome an obstacle is to tackle it head-on?

Are you confident in yourself and your decisions?

It's often easy to doubt yourself, but do you stand strong in the face of uncertainty? Do you have faith in your abilities and trust yourself to make the right decisions? Do you think that self-assurance is essential for success?

Do you take charge and take control?

A true leader can take charge and lead. Do you have the ability to make decisions quickly to get things done? Do you have confidence in your judgment and take charge of the situation?

Are you competitive?

While competition should not be taken to extremes, do you strive to be the best? Do you take pride in your accomplishments and want to do better than before?

Do you tend to be assertive and focused?

Getting tasks done requires an assertive attitude and focus. Can you remain calm and composed under pressure? Do you think that success requires unwavering concentration?

Do you look for solutions rather than problems?

Having a problem-solving mentality is essential. Do you look for creative ways to approach situations? Are you willing to think outside the box to find the best solution?

Answer these questions honestly to find out if Ogun is your divine parent. Whatever the answer, use this knowledge to deepen your understanding of Yoruba spirituality and build meaningful connections with your divine parent. Speaking with an elder or spiritual practitioner in the Yoruba tradition may also be useful to gain insight into your divine parent. With knowledge and understanding, you can tap into extraordinary levels of personal power and spiritual growth.

Key to the Quiz

Now that you've taken the quiz, it's time to see if Ogun is your divine parent. If you answered yes to most of the questions, Ogun will likely be your divine parent. He is a strong leader who embodies strength, courage, action, and innovation. He encourages you to take risks, be resilient in the face of adversity, and take charge of your life. You can use the power of Ogun to reach your goals and achieve greatness.

On the other hand, if you answered no to most of the questions, then Ogun is not likely to be your divine parent. However, that doesn't mean he isn't part of your spiritual journey. Ogun's energy can be called upon to help you overcome obstacles, find solutions, and become a leader in your own life. Even if he is not your divine parent, understanding Ogun's energy can still be beneficial in guiding you on the right path. Here's a deeper look at what Ogun represents, so you can use his energy to your advantage.

1. Challenges

Ogun is not one to shy away from a challenge. He's willing to take risks, often finding himself in tight spots with no clear solution in sight. But that's exactly why Ogun takes on such tasks. He loves the thrill and adrenaline of pushing the limits and pressing beyond his boundaries. In the end, it only enhances his growth as both an individual and a leader, giving him greater insight, stronger skills, and more resolve. As someone who is always looking to better himself, Ogun embraces these challenging situations with confidence and optimism.

2. Resilience

Ogun, the god of both war and creation, epitomizes resilience in many ways. He was born of thunder and then forged his path through battle. This example of determination to never give up is something everyone can strive for. Sometimes failure is inevitable, and getting back up and fighting can be difficult after you fall short. But with a bit of Ogun's spirit, hope, determination, and action-oriented progress, you can all build your path to success and develop an unwavering sense of resilience. After all, Ogun was full of knowledge, courage, and strength, something you can tap into as well when times get tough!

3. Risk Taking

Ogun is a real go-getter who's always looking out for new opportunities and embracing risks when they come his way. This can-do attitude has helped him succeed in his career, relationships, and hobbies. Whether it's building a business, learning something new, or pursuing a romantic interest, he won't be intimidated by obstacles or the possibility of failure. His ability to recognize the potential outcomes of his decisions and choose the paths with more worthy rewards has opened many doors for him and will surely continue leading him to greater accomplishments. He's an inspiration for everyone!

4. Leadership

Ogun is an inspirational leader who confidently guides his team toward success. He understands that a strong, confident presence is key to motivating and encouraging others, and he applies this to his leadership style. Ogun also understands that trust must be part of any successful team dynamic and works hard to ensure everyone feels comfortable enough to voice ideas and opinions. He leads with integrity, fairness, and wisdom, demonstrating how those qualities are essential components of good leadership. Ultimately, he is someone that you can look up to as an example of what true leadership should be.

5. Conflict

Ogun always hits the bull's eye when it comes to dealing with conflicts, showing his honest and direct approach. He's not one for beating around the bush and prefers to navigate these kinds of situations head-on in a friendly manner. This can often lead to a surprisingly peaceful outcome as he has an incredible knack for understanding both sides of the argument and finding common ground that everybody can agree on. Ogun is highly valued by those around him thanks to his diplomatic conflict resolution style, which almost always ends in a win-win scenario for everyone.

6. Confidence

Ogun is one inspiring god! He consistently sets goals for himself and has all the confidence he needs to accomplish them. Ogun's self-belief gives him the strength to face any challenge head-on, and he doesn't take no for an answer. That's why you can always count on him when times are difficult. His unwavering assurance in himself and positive attitude keep him going no matter what. He is someone to look up to in terms of confidence and perseverance, and he demonstrates that anything is indeed possible with enough drive and passion.

7. Control

Ogun is known for being a take-charge kind of god. If there's ever a difficult situation, he'll always do his best to be the one in control. His determination and resourcefulness make him an excellent leader who can find order even in the most chaotic moments. He has the confidence to make tough decisions and inspires those around him to keep pushing forward no matter what they face. You're lucky to have someone like Ogun to pray to. His composure and resilience help you out of tricky spots time and time again!

8. Competition

Ogun is the epitome of a modern, successful individual. He always aims high and gives his all in every endeavor, striving to reach goals with genuine ambition. However, what truly sets him apart is his unique ability to know when it's time for competition to give way to collaboration. He understands the importance of teamwork among peers and when tackling larger initiatives. Not only does it make things easier for everyone involved, but it also encourages others to step up and be part of the whole process. When Ogun puts aside individual pride and instead focuses on a collective end goal, amazing things often happen, which just goes to show how powerful working together can be!

9. Assertiveness

Ogun is a strongly assertive god who knows how to prioritize what matters most. He is adept at tackling tasks with a clear focus, getting in the right mindset, and never wavering until completion. His approach toward projects fosters a sense of efficiency as well as a great teamwork spirit. His no-nonsense attitude combined with a friendly demeanor helps him remain calm and composed while still efficiently making his voice heard among the team. Ogun's assertiveness is something that should be admired and thought of fondly, providing a much-needed dose of enthusiasm for people to bond over.

10. Solutions

Ogun takes a unique approach when it comes to problem-solving, always looking for solutions instead of dwelling on the negative. By taking this optimistic outlook, Ogun often stumbles on great opportunities that otherwise wouldn't have been noticed. Adopting the same perspective can make all the difference in terms of creating positive change in any situation and can often yield much more than expected results. You could take a page out of Ogun's book and take a shot at problem-solving with an optimistic attitude!

Deepening Your Understanding of Ogun

Delving deeper into Ogun can be a powerful way to connect with your sense of identity and spirituality. Whether you're seeking to learn more about the Yoruba culture in which he originates or is looking to channel his energies as part of your spiritual practice, studying Ogun can lead to a wealth of new knowledge and wisdom. As an Orisha and quintessential warrior, devotees worldwide have found power from connecting with his presence during times of transformation or upheaval. With research, rituals, and dedication, understanding Ogun can be hugely rewarding and enriching for anyone looking for a glimpse into the depths of African spirituality.

A. Ogun's Relationship with Change

Ogun is a fascinating African deity, often associated with a change in the Igbo tradition. He symbolizes both a beneficial and powerful force of growth, embracing transformations and helping humans to break through obstacles. Ogun can also provide protection during times of turmoil and stress, offering wisdom on tackling life's biggest challenges. This makes him a valuable figure for those looking to adjust their lives for the better or overcome difficult transitions. He may not be the most recognizable or popular deity, but this allows followers to truly appreciate his unique perspective and learn from his experiences of living through major shifts in understanding.

B. Ogun and Adaptability

Ogun embodies adaptability and resilience, two traits we all could use more of during these uncertain times. Ogun teaches us to look past the surface level of things and see the potential future waiting to be unlocked through creative solutions. This could mean altering your approach or viewpoints, finding new ways to interact with the world around you, and letting go of the status quo. With Ogun's guidance, you can better navigate these ever-changing tides in life and become empowered agents of change within yourself, your communities, and your environment alike.

C. Ogun and Taking Action

Ogun, the great Yoruba god of iron and war, reminds us to take action. It's easy to get stuck in the same routine, feeling like you are on a hamster wheel where day after day can blur into one long slog. But Ogun is here to tell you that just because something has been done before does not mean it cannot be improved. This can apply to any part of your life, from making small changes to spark joy in your everyday life to standing up and speaking out against injustice whenever possible. Making an effort to take action each day gives us a sense of accomplishment while helping us reach our goals and improve the world around us. By embracing Ogun's energy, you can work together toward improving yourself and your community with passion and determination.

D. Ogun and Courage

Ogun, the noble orisha of Yoruba mythology, is known as a brave warrior. He symbolizes strength and valor in the face of adversity, being a pillar of strength to whom we turn in moments of despair. Ogun gives you courage and fortitude to trudge through difficult times. He's a symbol of protection, too. His presence can be felt all around you every time you go on a difficult journey, every time you strive for success against great odds, and even when something appears impossible, but you still summon the inner strength to try, nonetheless. You should always remember Ogun, the brave spirit who embodies courage within everyone.

E. Ogun and Overcoming Adversity

Adversity comes in all shapes and sizes, and it can be daunting to face it. However, the Yoruba deity Ogun provides hope to those struggling against it. The god of iron, warfare, and labor champions those who strive to overcome their difficulties despite the odds. As long as you stay strong and persevere, Ogun will help you reach your goals. Whether it's conquering a battle or completing a project, this spirit offers unwavering strength and courage to reach peace and success. So, if you are facing an obstacle or have recently gone through a tribulation, remember that with Ogun supporting you, better days lie ahead!

How to Identify Your Divine Parent

Knowing which divine parent you are blessed with is an astonishing feeling. It helps shape who you are, giving you insight into what makes your character unique. Identifying your divine parent is easier than you might think. All it takes is a little honest introspection and being open to the answers that come. Start by thinking about what wisdom and skills come naturally to you. What do you feel passionate about or have an exceptional understanding of? Also, consider how your relationships have formed. Are there any particular gods or goddesses that always seem to attract your attention or influence in your life? Once these questions have been answered, doing some research into the gods presented can give more clarity on whether they could be your divine parent. Ultimately, no one can tell you who your divine parent is. You can take this extraordinary journey only by connecting to yourself and trusting in yourself.

This chapter discussed the concept of divine parenting in African spirituality and how Ogun, the great Yoruba god of iron and war, embodies courage and strength in difficult times. The quiz is provided as a tool to help you zero in on Ogun's personality traits and characteristics, as well as how to identify your divine parent. Hopefully, this chapter has provided insight and clarity into the power of divine parenting and explained how to connect with Ogun. Ultimately, it is up to you to connect with yourself and discover who holds this special place in your life. People should all strive to embrace Ogun's energy and work together towards a more peaceful, prosperous world.

Chapter 4: Ogun in Myths and Legends

Ogun is an influential Orisha, esteemed in the Yoruba religious tradition. Ogun has no single form or appearance. Instead, the deity encompasses a complex and multifaceted range of characteristics. The powerful and multifaceted deity is known as a warrior and protector and is associated with justice and loyalty. In addition to these roles, Ogun also governs conflict, purity, blacksmithing, metalworking, hunting, and agriculture, among other areas. His spirit embodies courage, strength, and transformation.

Ogun is associated with many forms, including a warrior and protector.
Wood, J. G. (John George), CC BY-SA 4.0 <https://creativecommons.org/licenses/by-sa/4.0>, via Wikimedia Commons https://commons.wikimedia.org/wiki/File:African_Warriors_Skirmish.jpg

Considering all his many responsibilities and abilities, it's not surprising that devotees give thanks to Ogun for providing them with protection in this life. This chapter will overview Ogun's origin, his paths, and the different legends and stories that portray him as a powerful being. It will also explore his relationship with Olodumare, the Supreme Being in the Yoruba pantheon. By the end of this chapter, you should have a better understanding of Ogun and the role he plays in Yoruba culture.

Overview of Ogun

Ogun is a fascinating deity who is said to have been the first Orisha to come from heaven. He descended with his machete and forged a path through the wilderness for humans to follow, thus allowing humankind's progress. Ogun developed tools and weapons out of metal, tamed the wilderness, and gave people access to knowledge that allowed them to prosper. Ogun is revered as the god of metal and is often associated with blacksmithing, war, hunting, and labor.

The Origin Story of Ogun

Ogun is the chief Yoruba deity of iron and warfare, a powerful figure of ingenuity and invention. He is often seen as a messenger, liaising between the gods and humans, as he is connected to mankind and the gods. Ogun's origin story goes back to ancient times when he emerged from a calabash planted on the bank of the northern Niger River. He is said to be small inside the calabash but powerful, representing hope and prosperity of becoming something greater. Ogun's message is still honored today, and his mythology remains integral to Yoruba folklore, inspiring their people even centuries later.

Paths of Ogun

The Paths of Ogun, an African symbol of power and strength, have long been a key source of inspiration for many. Imbued with perseverance and determination, the powerful spirit of Ogun has been a beacon that beckons us forward on life's journey. In some traditions, Ogun is also associated with justice and insightfulness, thus a pillar of support when facing difficult decisions. At their core, the Paths of Ogun show followers that though life may have its twists and turns, they always have their inner guide to return to in times of strife. So, if you ever need inspiration along your path, take comfort in knowing the Paths of Ogun are ever-present to light your way in times of darkness.

Ogun worshipers sure know how to honor their deities! By singing Ogun's oríkì (a powerful greeting in hymns/mantras, etc.), worshippers proclaim their appreciation for this powerful Yoruba god. One line that carries so much weight is: "Ògún ó tí bá rè sílé sílẹ́" which translates to "Ògún is in seven paths." This term reflects an understanding of the god as a pathfinder or one with unrivaled access to all routes. Essentially, it reminds followers that Ogun is everywhere, heading up growth and progress with each step he makes across the seven paths!

1. Oggun Alagbo

The paths of Ogun Meji comprise many ancient rituals and traditions unique to the religion, originating from Ifá, a traditional Yoruba divination system. Oggun Alagbo is a powerful deity highly respected by those in the blacksmith profession. Known as the patron of blacksmiths, he exemplifies hard work and dedication, toiling endlessly from night to day. He may come across as harsh and fearful at times, but this strong personality has helped forge Oggun into a symbol of strength for those in his field. Worshipped alongside Yemaya Okute, his wife, Oggun's presence can be seen throughout smithing communities who recognize him according to various names such as Alaguede, Alagbo, and Alagbede.

2. Oggun Onile

Oggun Onile is a fascinating spirit renowned for its connection to the realm of land and exploration. This spirit brings with it feelings of comfort and security when connected to the home, but it also holds the promise of unveiling vast discoveries. Oggun Onile's wisdom can be seen in his ability to recognize the potential in unmapped regions, allowing him to traverse the land like no other. It is no surprise why this spirit is so beloved. From his ability to provide a stable foundation to inviting encouragement for growth, Oggun Onile celebrates stability and potential. Whether through physical travel or inner self-reflection, this spirit takes great delight in your open spirit of discovery and gives you the courage to take on life's challenges with boldness and assurance.

3. Oggun Meji

Oggun Meji represents strength and communication within oneself and the community, an understanding that strife can occur without balance within our communities and us. This path focuses on sacrifices given to balance the needs of humans and nature, allowing them to live in harmony. The practice of meditation helps humans to understand how they exist in the world. It helps them see their place among others and also understand themselves better by listening carefully and responding thoughtfully. By paying close attention to Oggun Meji's teachings, anyone can find a sense of peace and connection with themselves as well as the world around them.

4. Oggun Oloyon

Oggun Oloyon is the most well-known of all Ogun's paths because it is here that the story of how he became the god of metal originated. It tells of how a farmer was having trouble clearing his land, as every time he tried to do so, his tools kept breaking. In frustration, he made a plea to the gods, and Ogun answered his call. Ogun used his tools to clear the land in mere moments, thus earning him the title of "the god of metal."

5. Oggun Irumole

Oggun Irumole is a powerful spirit who embodies protection and guidance. He can be seen as the guardian of travelers on a journey, helping them to stay safe and find their way home. This spirit also works to protect individuals from evil influences and negative energies while guarding homes against robbery and burglary. Ogun Irumole also lends a hand in matters of love, such as helping heal broken hearts and opening up communication channels between two people.

6. Oggun Oyeku Meji

Oggun Oyeku Meji is the spirit of war, conflict, and courage. This path emphasizes the importance of standing up for justice when needed and having the courage to face one's fears and fight for something one believes in. Oggun Oyeku Meji teaches followers that victory comes through hard work and perseverance, reminding them to never give up on their dreams no matter how difficult the path ahead may be. He also reminds them of the necessity of protecting those who are weaker and standing up for what is right.

7. Oggun Akomi

The Ogun Akomi path embodies the spirit of healing and creativity. This spirit works to inspire individuals to practice their unique gifts and express themselves creatively, helping them appreciate the beauty in every aspect of life. He encourages followers to have faith in their abilities and push beyond any boundaries that may prevent them from achieving greatness. Additionally, Ogun Akomi is a symbol of hope, offering comfort in times of difficulty and reminding followers to always look toward the future with optimism.

Legends and Stories about Ogun

Legends and stories about the God Ogun are plentiful in West African culture. This deity of metalworking, war, and hunting is believed to have many facets, including the ability to bring fortune, create powerful tools for those with the skill to wield them, and protect those who honor him. In some versions of the mythologies surrounding Ogun, he is portrayed as a trickster who uses his knowledge of powers to outwit his opponents or even fellow Gods. Because of this, these stories are just as much about ethical dilemmas as they are about wisdom found through his teachings. Legends about Ogun make for fascinating tales that may illustrate lessons on bravery, strength, and justice that can still be embraced today.

1. Ogun and Yemaya

Ogun and Yemaya are very prominent deities in Yoruba culture. Ogun is the god of iron, warriors, and hunters and is said to be ever-present in times of warfare and death. Yemaya is the great mothering spirit, often shown with a crown of shells on her head, who provides guidance and protection to those seeking it. Both of these deities have fascinating stories associated with them. From tales about how Ogun created the world to festivals sponsored by Yemaya for her followers, these legends are timeless reminders of these figures' central role in Yoruba mythology. Whether you're looking for guidance on your spiritual journey or just curious about the legends that make up this cultural tradition, learning more about Ogun and Yemaya can be an enlightening adventure!

2. The Story of the Talking Stone

Many stories and legends exist about Ogun, the Yoruba God of Iron and War. One of the most popular is that of the talking stone. According to legend, when Ogun seeks to hear words of counsel on a particular issue, he visits a talking stone found in the Ira forest. When he arrives at the forest and kneels before the stone, it begins to speak with divine knowledge, offering advice on his journey. This story's variations span West Africa and even beyond geographical borders, proving how this cherished tale has ingrained itself into the culture. Even today, communities continue to be charmed by the story of Ogun and his magical talking stone!

3. The Suitors Tale

Ogun is a god of many stories and legends, especially concerning his relationship with the suitors who pursue him. According to one tale, Ogun had no home long ago and was looking for a place to stay. Every evening he would arrive in a new village hoping to find kindness and shelter. Instead, he would be met with disdain and rejection. One night, despite being turned away from three consecutive households, Ogun found comfort when an anonymous benefactor opened their door and welcomed him in for restful sleep. Whether this legend was based on fact or fiction remains unknown to us today. However, it serves as an example of how much the people of ancient times admired Ogun's resilience and bravery against adversity.

4. Ogun and Osun

Ogun and Osun are two fascinating gods from the Yoruba religion of Nigeria. Ogun's stories tell of a powerful, brave warrior figure who could also be extremely creative. The most popular story tells the tale of how he discovered ironworking to help his people build tools, weapons, and other important items in their daily lives. Osun, on the other hand, is the goddess of beauty and feminine love. According to legend, she brings abundance and fertility to people's lives. She uses her beauty as a source of inspiration for many art forms, including painting, poetry, music, and dance. Stories around Osun often revolve around romance between people or between different gods or goddesses. Regardless of the story type, Ogun and Osun play an important role in Yoruba culture.

5. Ogun and the Forest of Truth

Ogun is a powerful figure in West African folklore, often depicted as a warrior and blacksmith. He is broadly associated with justice, truth, and protection, the three values that were highly prized during the period in which the myth of Ogun originated. Ogun's most prominent story takes place in the Forest of Truth, where he embarks on an epic journey to receive guidance from his ancestors. As Anansi, the spider, says: "Ogun is no ordinary feat. He marched through woods unknown, searching for his father's lore, and left with a knowledge greater than before." This classic story serves as an ode to the pursuit of resilience, strength, and understanding. These are values followers can all take away from when exploring stories centered on Ogun.

6. Ogun and Eleggua

Ogun and Eleggua are revered figures in African folklore, with countless legends and stories devoted to them. Ogun is associated with war and skillful weapon smithing, while Eleggua's purpose was to serve as a messenger between the spiritual realm and humankind. Together they were regarded as two of the most influential gods of old African cultures, with celebrated stories detailing their fascinating adventures.

Tales of mighty battles between Ogun and the trickster deity Eshu offer insights into how African societies viewed victory and defeat. Furthermore, the characteristics associated with Eleggua of mischievousness, cunningness, and cleverness have been celebrated for generations in African story-telling. If you're looking for exciting tales to bring history to life, look no further than the legends of Ogun and Eleggua.

7. The Battle of the Beavers

Legends and stories about Ogun and the battle of the Beavers are part of many cultures, but most commonly those originating from Western Africa. Ogun is credited with fighting off the beavers who were trying to take over the forests. The legend usually goes that he leads his troops into battle against the beavers and eventually defeats them. The stories vary slightly depending on the culture, but generally, it is held up as an example of courage and perseverance in making sure that humans retain control over their environment. It's a cautionary tale against greed and lust for power, urging followers not to let their desires take away their resources or burden them with too much work. In that sense, this legend has left a lasting impression on humankind throughout the ages.

8. Ogun and the Seven Leaf Clover

Ogun is an influential figure in many African religious traditions, and one of the most iconic symbols associated with him is the seven-leaf clover. These seven leaves are meant to represent the seven paths of life that Ogun laid out, and each has its own story attached to it. Legends tell of Ogun traveling around his kingdom, teaching people about these paths and about how precious freedom was. Other stories center on Ogun as a powerful warrior who won battles with superhuman strength. While the truth of these stories may be up for debate, they show us how deeply Ogun has been a part of African culture throughout history – and why his symbol of the seven-leaf clover continues to be held in high regard today.

9. Ogun and the White Robe

Ogun is one of the most beloved characters in African folklore. One of his many stories involves a mighty battle with a spirit wearing a white robe. Ogun had to accomplish two tasks before being crowned king: 1) taking possession of the white robe and 2) beating the spirit. His courage, intelligence, and strength helped him succeed, setting an example for future generations. Ogun is also well-known for his role as the god of war, iron, and technology, so it's no wonder he has become such an influential figure throughout history. Today, he is remembered as a powerful hero who challenges injustice and evil wherever they may be found. Although his stories are rooted in legend, his qualities remain timeless and can inspire everyone!

10. The Legend of Oshun River

The legend of the Oshun River is full of deep mystique and exciting stories and tales. In the mythology of the Ogun people, stories are handed down through generations to explain why things occur in nature. It is believed that Oshun River has been blessed by the God Ogun, who resides atop its banks and looks out for his people. Ogun is considered to be an ironsmith who creates tools for warriors to use in battle, but he also serves as a protector who generously showers his followers with blessings. He is famous for challenging death, rescuing innocent souls from harm's way, and helping bring justice whenever injustice was found. Followers believe that anyone who respects Ogun properly will be rewarded with protection and good fortune. These legends offer a unique insight into the Oshun River's history and its inhabitants' culture while captivating listeners with incredible stories.

It is believed that the Oshun River is blessed by Ogun.
https://www.pexels.com/photo/body-of-water-between-green-leaf-trees-709552/

Ogun and Olodumare

Ogun and Olodumare are two of the most important deities of Yoruba culture. Ogun is revered as a great spirit of knowledge and strength, while Olodumare is seen as the highest deity, having created all things and whose power surpasses any other spirits or forces. This relationship between Ogun and Olodumare is fundamental in the practice of Yoruba spiritualism as they are thought to be inseparable energies that work within your life. They are understood to often have complementary roles, balancing your spiritual experience. It's incredible to reflect upon how these powerful gods remain relevant today!

Significance of Ogun's Relationship with Olodumare

Yoruba mythology tells a fascinating story of the relationship between Ogun and Olodumare. Deeply intertwined in the stories about creation and the order of life is an understanding of how the two worked together to bring about powerful change for those who believed in them. As a powerful elemental god, Ogun ensured Olodumare's creations were developed by his plan. Ogun is said to be a skilled metalworker who taught humans how to work with iron and smelt it into weapons and tools. His teachings were essential to help humans decimate the Earth's resources while ensuring they could build civilizations from scratch. Many followers of Yoruba mythology will point out that Olodumare would have been lost without Ogun's influence over human development. The world's modern advances owe much to this duo's partnership!

Olodumare's Role in Ogun's Legend

In the legend of Ogun and Olodumare, Olodumare plays a critical role in delivering a valuable lesson. Ogun, the warrior-king, ventures out on a quest to find solace after losing his wife and children. His journey leads him to meet Olodumare, the All-Pervading One. Through this divine encounter, Ogun grows spiritually as he learns humility and faith, and surrenders to the will of Olodumare. This powerful lesson encourages followers to be steadfast in their belief that justice and mercy come from our Creator above all else. Ultimately, Ogun's story proves that when you give everything to Olodumare, his grace will produce positive life-changing results.

Symbolic Meaning of Ogun's Connection to Olodumare

Ogun, a force that works to make change and progress, is also closely connected to Olodumare, the supreme creative being in the universe. While Ogun's might and strength are meant to stand out and make an impact, it is only through his relationship with Olodumare that he can fulfill that purpose.

Symbolically, the connection indicates the importance of understanding where your power comes from and keeping it grounded in something greater. If it is not underpinned by your connection to your deity and their cosmic plan, then there can be no true transformation or growth. Understanding this partnership between Ogun and Olodumare shines great insight into our own lived experience. You may have strength, but if you're not present with your spiritual connection and have layer upon layer of self-reflection, you'll never truly reach your highest potential.

Ogun in Other Worlds and Religions

Ogun is often seen as a heroic figure in religious and mythical stories, ranging from West African folktales to Russian epics and beyond. Represented through different symbolisms depending on the origin story, Ogun is revered across the world for his strength and determination. Like many gods of power, he is often associated with weapons such as swords or spears. In addition, he stands out from other gods worldwide because of his ability to teach people skills in craftsmanship and blacksmithing, an essential skill in societies throughout time. Overall, it's awe-inspiring how Ogun's presence has been preserved and celebrated through the ages!

Significance of Ogun in Afro-Cuban Spirituality

Ogun is also a significant Afro-Cuban spiritual figure representing strength and passion. He is honored as one of the most powerful armed warriors and is believed to open any door that has been closed. Ogun is seen as a patron for those seeking their freedom, whether physical or spiritual. He encourages Cubans to move forward with courage, allowing them to develop connections between their past and the present. For this reason, many devout people continue to pay homage to him today by lighting candles in his honor or reciting prayers in the name of Ogun on special occasions.

Ogun is among the most timeless and highly celebrated deities in many different cultures worldwide. As a god of strength, courage, and passion, he is often seen as the forerunner of progress and change. His connection to Olodumare reinforces the importance of understanding where true power comes from and how your spiritual practices can be used to reach a higher potential. His heroic deeds continue to inspire people worldwide, as his stories remain part of the collective history and culture. Through this shared understanding, you can honor Ogun in all his greatness!

Chapter 5: What Ogun Teaches His Followers

Ogun is an influential figure for many, both spiritually and historically. If you take the time to learn, his experiences are filled with valuable lessons showing you how to live in the world. Ogun's life taught him to adapt and embrace change with courage and strength. He also embodied kindness towards others, especially those who were as displaced as he was. Every attempt at reinvention requires resilience, but when you look at it through the lens of someone like Ogun, it also carries promise and possibility. The spiritual legacy of Ogun gives followers hope that even when faced with such uncertainty, there is beauty in reimagining what your life can become.

Embarking on a journey through the paths of Ogun, the Yoruba god of iron and technology, can be intimidating, exciting, and ultimately enlightening. Each step you take will help you discover your unique place in the world, whether that is understanding your creative skills, exploring career paths, or learning to overcome personal challenges. You can also gather the experiences necessary to break down barriers and build bridges between people and communities by pushing through difficult terrain. The search for identity is a crucial quest for many people, but Ogun's path may offer you something even greater, a gateway to creating your future.

This chapter will explore the eight Paths of Ogun further and how we can use them as inspiration to guide us on our paths. It will discuss the importance of the preservation of knowledge, traveling and movement, strength, communication, helping others, spiritual awakening, courage, and finally, healing and creativity. By the end of this chapter, you'll better understand each path and how it can be applied in our everyday lives.

Oggun Alagbo - The Path of Elderly Wisdom

Oggun Alagbo is the path that celebrates the value of wisdom through age. It encourages you to step into your role as an elder, leader, and teacher with clarity and conviction, and it highlights the necessity of relying on years of experience to guide you through life's complex challenges. Oggun Alagbo reminds people that if they embrace their human history without fear or apprehension, accepting who they were in the past while embracing their future with open arms, they can rise above any obstacle. This ancient path sheds light on how you can use knowledge learned over a lifetime to leave a lasting mark on the world.

Oggun Alagbo encourages the value of wisdom through experience and age.
https://www.pexels.com/photo/two-woman-looking-on-persons-bracelet-667203/

A. The Importance of Preservation of Knowledge

Preserving knowledge and wisdom is something that many cultures have done through the years, and one good example of this is Oggun Alagbo, or "the path of elderly wisdom." This Nigerian tradition emphasizes the wisdom of respecting and seeking out the advice and knowledge of elders in our communities. It serves as a reminder to all that knowledge never becomes obsolete. Regardless of how experienced or well-educated somebody may be, there is always something else to learn from those with greater understanding, life experience, and knowledge than them. Keeping these traditions alive ensures that generations before you are remembered and celebrated for their contributions to your shared human experience.

B. Finding Your Own Path with Oggun Alagbo

Oggun Alagbo is an amazing opportunity to find your path and learn from the insights of experienced, wise elders. Learning from those who have come before us and understanding their perspective gives us a much clearer look at our paths and guidance that sometimes only the wisdom acquired over time can provide. Through the inspirational teachings of Oggun Alagbo, you can recognize your destiny and take steps towards achieving it with newfound clarity. Embark on this journey and embrace the growth and enlightenment this process can bring.

C. Appreciating the Power of Elders

Appreciating the power of elders is both a humbling and enlightening experience. Oggun Alagbo, which translates to The Path of Elderly Wisdom in West African Yoruba, shines a unique light on the motivations behind this appreciation. It suggests that ancient wisdom often gives us perspective, regardless of how turbulent or unclear our world may seem. This wisdom may be attained by seeking out elders in their community who share their stories and experiences to gain knowledge and insights into facing life's most trying times with grace and strength.

Embracing the power of elders can help us expand our horizons beyond what we thought possible while holding fast to the traditions passed down from generation to generation. By paying homage to those that have gone before, you are gifted with an invaluable resource for growth in both your personal and professional life.

Oggun Onile - The Path of Traveling and Movement

Oggun Onile, or the Yoruba path of traveling and movement, has been around for centuries. It is a fascinating exploration into the spiritual aspects of movement and how different cultures from around the world approach human interactions on the go. In Yoruba culture specifically, Oggun Onile is a belief system that centers on ensuring one's safety while traveling and emphasizes the importance of clear communication in interpersonal relationships.

It also focuses on building harmony between those with varying superstitions. Oggun Onile practices often involve revealing physical symbols to signify safe passage while traveling and an openness to discuss any pressing issues respectfully. This ancient belief system provides insight into how different societies have coped with what could have been very difficult journeys like traveling long distances on foot or at sea.

A. Embracing Adaptability with Oggun Onile

Oggun Onile is a unique path of traveling and movement embraced by the Yoruba people that focuses on adaptability. This philosophy involves understanding your environment, using it to your advantage, and staying fluid to move in the best direction for your growth. Practicing this method can give you real benefits, such as improved navigation and navigation-based problem-solving skills. On top of that, developing an appreciation for how environments can affect your life fosters a more dynamic mindset and allow you to prepare yourself better when faced with change or challenges. Learning to embrace adaptability through Oggun Onile may be just what you need to get ahead in life.

B. Going Out into the World to Seek Opportunity

For anyone interested in seeking opportunity, the Yoruba path of traveling and movement, Oggun Onile, is a great way to embark on the journey of discovering what lies beyond. This practice can provide insight into the challenges which may come up while stepping out into the world, along with how to work through them. It involves having faith in oneself and one's journey, creating a system of support among close family and friends as one embarks on different life experiences, and realizing that no matter what challenges arise, one will navigate them skillfully. In times when it may not seem easy, listening to the voice of intuition within oneself can make all the difference.

C. Utilizing Self-Reliance to Forge Your Path

Oggun Onile is an ancient and powerful philosophy. In essence, it is a path of self-reliance that encourages individuals to take charge of their lives, forge their paths and break away from conventional thinking. Oggun Onile urges its adherents to seek deeper understanding and insight into life by becoming better communicators, establishing greater connections with their environment, and mastering the creative self-expression necessary for personal growth.

By learning this ancient wisdom, each person has the potential to bring peace and harmony into their lives, as well as enhance their health and well-being. Embracing Oggun Onile grants you greater freedom when deciding how you'll approach your travels through life and create your unique path with courage, confidence, and strength.

Oggun Meji - The Path of Strength and Communication

Oggun Meji is a powerful path originating among the Yoruba people, who worship deities representing different forces of nature. Along this path, individuals explore strength and communication through metaphysical practices deeply embedded in their ancestral roots. Oggun Meji instills meaningful insight into life's daily struggles and encourages adherents to strive for inner peace and balance.

Through spiritual rituals, including medicine circles, drumming sessions, and offerings to pot shamanism, one can develop a stronger sense of self, open communication channels within their community, and cultivate greater awareness about their environment. By cultivating inner strength through Oggun Meji, you can establish effective healing relationships with fellow humans and deepen your connection to the surrounding world.

A. Taking Action to Better Yourself with Oggun Meji

Oggun Meji is a powerful Yoruba path of strength and communication that can help you better yourself in many different areas. This ancient practice holds the secrets to unlocking what's holding you back and equipping you with the strength, courage, and wisdom to take action at any time. Within this path lies powerful rituals, affirmations, and meditations to help guide you on your spiritual journey and manifest your desired life. These teachings will help support your spiritual goals and provide practical advice on how to recognize and push through any obstacles preventing personal growth.

B. Understanding the Power of Words and Expression

Oggun Meji provides insight into the power of words and how they can be used both positively and negatively to shape our lives, relationships, and circumstances. Oggun Meji teaches us how to use our communicative abilities strategically to effectively share our thoughts and feelings better while avoiding misunderstandings. Through this traditional practice, you learn how to exercise good judgment during important conversations and begin to repair damaged bonds by using sincere words with love, sincerity, respect, and understanding. By speaking directly from the heart to those you care about most, you can reach a level of mutual understanding which will benefit all sides long-term.

C. Learning to Harness the Strength within You

Oggun Meji teaches you to recognize and access your power within, allowing you to navigate through life's challenges with clarity and grace. Oggun Meji's guiding principles include introspection and self-reflection, embracing innate strengths, accepting the truth, and recognizing boundaries. Through these practices, you can harness the force of your inner voice, allowing it to guide you through difficult situations while maintaining peace of mind in both success and failure. As you become more attuned to this path of strength and communication, you can become your own most authentic self with greater ease.

Oggun Oloyon - The Path of Helping Others

Oggun Oloyon is a Yoruba path that encourages us to help others above all else. Genuine service is paramount, whether it's with tangible items, advice, or support. It resonates with a strong sense of community where everyone works together to preserve harmony in their families and neighborhoods. Oggun Oloyon allows you to practice being selfless even if there may be no immediate reward, as it's been said that "helping people in need makes all your actions more meaningful." Although this may be an ancient tradition, you can adopt and apply it in your daily life for its timelessness and relevance.

A. The Value of Compassion with Oggun Oloyon

Oggun Oloyon is an ancient Yoruba tradition that values compassion and helping others as an integral part of a meaningful life. This path recognizes your interdependence with each other, encourages you to be helpful and generous, and allows you to form meaningful connections both within your community and beyond. Oggun Oloyon is rooted in the belief that there is fulfillment in giving rather than taking or accumulating material possessions. By engaging in acts of care and generosity, you can experience greater joy in your life, feel connected to others, and bring about positive change. Practicing compassion makes you a healthier individual, builds stronger communities, and, ultimately a better world for everyone.

B. Understanding the Power of Kindness

Oggun Oloyon, or the Path of Helping Others, is an ancient philosophy of kindness that connects to the spirit of humanity and its importance in personal development. Oggun Oloyon comprises the idea that your spirituality and well-being will flourish if you strive to understand those around you and empathize with their struggles. Invoking this concept means it is your responsibility to care for others through material items or financial support and acts of love and compassion.

For example, think about a time when you shared a comforting conversation with someone who felt alone. That's a powerful act of kindness with deep spiritual significance for both of you. By recognizing your interconnectedness with each other and understanding how impactful careless gestures can be, you can start leveraging the power of Oggun Oloyon in your everyday life to spread more healing energy.

C. Utilizing Your Resources to Help Others

Oggun Oloyon, the Yoruba spiritual path of helping others, can be a powerful and rewarding way to aid those in need. It encourages you to use all physical and mental resources to extend assistance. From giving basic physical items, possessions, or money, to providing emotional support or caring services, it is possible to make a positive difference in everyone's lives. Understanding the importance of relationships and mutual interdependence makes it possible to serve with sincerity, patience, and humility while elevating our spiritual growth – and that of others.

Oggun Irumole - The Path of Spiritual Awakening

Oggun Irumole, the Yoruba spiritual path of awakening and transcendence, is an ancient practice that remains a powerful force today. It emphasizes developing a strong connection to the divine forces of nature while elevating spirituality through music, movement, prayer, and hieroglyphs. To stay true to its core values of knowledge, understanding, and respect for others, followers must abide by certain principles like the discipline of the mind and body, seeking inner peace, and understanding one's place in the universe.

Oggun Irumole teaches you how to access spiritual guidance from your ancestors and divine forces that lead you to open up new paths of self-transformation. Its long-lasting tradition of cultivating strong bonds between people from different cultures and backgrounds nurtures personal growth, which can only have positive consequences for present and future generations.

A. Growing with Oggun Irumole

Through Oggun Irumole's teachings, practitioners gain a new understanding of the basic principles of spirituality and learn how to wake up their own power. As part of this process, you are taught that knowledge is only partially found in books but must also come from experience for it to be truly meaningful. By learning more about this traditional practice and using it as guidance for spiritual growth, practitioners will discover a path to greater knowledge, intuition, and peace of mind.

B. Encouraging Self-Reflection and Improvement

Oggun Irumole is a practice that provides inspiring and meaningful encouragement to practice self-reflection and improvement. Through various techniques and rituals, this Yoruba spiritual path takes a holistic approach, helping practitioners to become more mindful of their thoughts, feelings, and behavior. It also helps you to better understand your strengths and weaknesses while developing inner peace, clarity, purpose, and motivation.

With its transformative potential, Oggun Irumole can be a powerful tool for those on the journey to self-improvement. Plus, the supportive community that often forms around this practice adds vital support from those with expert knowledge and experiences in the way of life. As a bonus, Oggun Irumole is highly adaptable, offering flexibility for individual or specific needs, so anyone can benefit from it regardless of what stage they're at in their lives.

C. Seeking Out Spiritual Growth

Oggun Irumole, the Yoruba path of spiritual awakening, offers a unique opportunity to seekers of spiritual growth. It is a deeply enriching experience that provides teachings to open your mind and soul and exercises the body through energetic rituals. Through this powerful practice of self-reflection, understanding one's inner truth and life purpose are revealed. And while there may be challenges on this journey of exploration and growth, the experiences gained from doing this work will guide you throughout life. Connect with Oggun Irumole today and witness how it can open up new pathways for enlightenment and give you a new perspective on life!

Oggun Oyeku Meji - The Path of Courage

Oggun Oyeku Meji is a powerful practice within the Yoruba tradition. Oggun Oyeku Meji is the path of courage and strength that comes from inner knowledge. It encourages individuals to be brave in overcoming fear and difficult emotions and find strength in their spiritual journeys. People who practice Oggun Oyeku Meji strive to have faith in themselves and trust themselves, even in seemingly impossible situations.

This ancient set of principles can bring courage and mental clarity to anyone who puts effort into understanding it properly. With greater self-awareness comes better decision-making, greater compassion for others, and a renewed spirit of fortitude. As you endure different challenges, Oggun Oyeku Meji can offer insight into how best to manage them while remaining connected with your inner resolve.

A. Embracing Change with Oggun Oyeku Meji

Embracing change can be challenging, especially when we aren't sure of the outcome. But embracing change with Oggun Oyeku Meji, a set of philosophical and spiritual principles, can help you work your way through change with courage and the belief that the result will be better than before. Oggun Oyeku Meji helps you push beyond your physical and mental boundaries and recognize that taking risks is okay while staying focused on your purpose. With this philosophy, change can be embraced and bring out the best in you as you step into new opportunities and face your fears head-on.

B. Learning to Overcome Fear

Ogun Oyeku Meji, or the Path of Courage, is an ancient meditation and visualization practice that helps you improve your courage and overcome fear. Positive affirmations make you feel strong, empowered, and confident in this practice. You learn to ground yourself in the present moment, let go of worry and anxiety, and find inner peace through intentional focus and relaxation techniques. With regular repetition, the ability to access your inner strength builds up so you can face fearful situations with greater resilience and poise. Through Ogun Oyeku Meji, you discover how easily your fears can be allayed as you align more with your highest potential for success.

C. Encouraging Self-Confidence and Determination

Oggun Oyeku Meji is an ancient practice that originated within the Yoruba culture, and its primary purpose is to give individuals the courage to increase their self-confidence and determination. This belief system combines purposeful movements, special mantras, proverbs, meditation, rhythmical clapping of hands, and visualizations. The idea behind this tradition is to reunite oneself with the higher power to strengthen self-identity in life's experiences and trials.

Those who practice Oggun Oyeku Meji believe it can provide resilience and emotional balance when facing difficult times by deepening people's connection with their spiritual essence. This practice has proven successful for generations of followers, invoking positive changes in behavior and beliefs regarding life's challenging moments. As a result of its spiritual support, Oggun Oyeku Meji leaves practitioners feeling empowered and ready to face any adversity head-on.

Oggun Akomi - The Path of Healing and Creativity

Oggun Akomi is a unique system of healing and creativity developed by the Yoruba people. While traditional Western medicine focuses on treating symptoms, this holistic approach sees health as an interconnected combination of mind, body, and spirit that must all be in balance to achieve optimal well-being. Combining traditional methods such as herbal remedies with activities such as singing, dancing, art therapy, storytelling, and divination, Oggun Akomi helps individuals identify and release physical, emotional, and spiritual blockages to achieve a deeper sense of connection with themselves.

Through its focus on creativity and self-expression, this practice offers communities a powerful tool for connecting with their ancestry while addressing present-day burdens. Oggun Akomi is transforming how you think about healing in a way that prioritizes growth over suffering, making it an invaluable pathway to discover a healthier, more vibrant life.

A. Appreciating the Power of Healing with Oggun Akomi

Oggun Akomi is an amazing practice that has been used for centuries to help its practitioners find peace and clarity. Through their combination of art, music, prayer, and reverence for ancestors and the divine spirit, Oggun Akomi creates a powerful healing journey of self-discovery. When embraced with an open heart and mind, this path of creativity and spiritual connection can bring about profound changes in one's life, from finding inner strength to unlocking untapped potential.

Oggun Akomi invites you to be present in the moment, appreciate your higher power, recognize the beauty that lies within yourself and create your own story through meaningful ritual practices. Its power lies in its ancient traditions and its ability to transform you by connecting you deeply with who you are at your core. There truly is nothing like it.

B. Learning How to Deal with Loss and Grief

Grief and loss can be incredibly painful to manage. But there's hope. The ancient practice of Oggun Akomi, based on the Yoruba understanding of healing and creativity, offers a unique approach to dealing with these complex emotions. It includes effective methods of managing the energy that comes along with grief and loss while honoring the individual's spirituality and values.

This path of healing takes into consideration an individual's unique background, view on life, and relationship with others while finding creative ways to manage strong feelings to avoid becoming overwhelmed by them. Anyone looking for an alternative way of managing grief or loss should consider exploring Oggun Akomi. It could offer clarity, direction, and peace through a traditional process meant for healing and creating lasting change in all aspects of life.

C. Using Creativity to Overcome Challenges

Oggun Akomi is a Yoruba path of healing and creativity that encourages individuals to solve their challenges creatively. Through this practice, you can identify the constructive power of your imagination, develop greater self-awareness, and learn to manage difficult moments. This involves learning the art of transforming raw thoughts into achievable goals while recognizing potential risks and threats to prevent future consequences.

Through Oggun Akomi, individuals gain the confidence they need to move forward and discover new ways to nurture their creativity and use it as a tool for problem-solving. With dedication and proper guidance, practitioners can practice Oggun Akomi to unlock their full potential, overcome obstacles with grace, and create a supportive environment for themselves along their journey toward healing and mental well-being.

Invoking Ogun in Everyday Life

Ogun is an incredibly powerful figure in the Yoruba pantheon, and his presence can be felt everywhere. In everyday life, you may invoke Ogun for any number of reasons, from protection to healing to insight, using traditional prayer and honorifics. This can be done at home at any time, although many adherents like to hold ceremonies before important events or transitions. It is said that Ogun can bring courage and strength to those he watches over while banishing obstacles out of their way. You can ask him to support and guide us through difficult journeys by calling upon his name with respect and reverence.

Here is a list of tips and tricks for invoking Ogun in everyday life:

- Offer prayers and honorifics to Ogun before important events or transitions
- Connect with the spirit of Ogun by calling him in moments of need - be it protection, healing, insight, or courage
- Stick to traditional prayer and honorifics when invoking the power of Ogun
- Spend time meditating on his role in your life and the lessons he teaches.
- Seek out guidance and support from experienced priests and priestesses when in doubt
- Remember to always show respect to Ogun and thank him for his guidance
- Find ways to express your gratitude for Ogun's help in your life

By following these simple tips and tricks, you can invite the spirit of Ogun into your life and benefit from his wisdom.

This chapter has presented Ogun's teachings through the paths of Akomi and Onile. Through Ogun's example, you can learn to show courage in the face of adversity and use your creativity to overcome any challenge. With respect and reverence, you can also invoke the power of Ogun to bring courage, strength, and guidance into your life. By following the tips and tricks mentioned here, you can benefit from

Ogun's wisdom and experience growth through healing, creativity, and spiritual understanding.

Chapter 6: Ogun's Symbols and Offerings

Ogun, the Orisha of iron and labor, is seen as a major deity across many parts of the world. He is known for his strength and unyielding determination; these traits were so honored that he was presented with the title "Ender of Difficulties." Ogun leads by example, inspiring those who revere him to work hard to meet their goals. An inventive god, he influences progress and encourages posterity. All who look toward Ogun for guidance can be sure that success will follow if they strive for excellence. He is an invaluable source of comfort and power during times of hardship, ever encouraging you to rise above your struggles.

Ogun is a complex deity with many facets, reflecting deep history and resonance in the African diaspora. He is associated with a wide variety of colors, animals, plants, crystals, symbols, and veves. Each has a distinct meaning that identifies the kind of energy Ogun wields. From the vibrant shades of crimson and maroon to powerful animals like the ram and rooster, each forms a connection between Ogun and the people who revere him. The plants representing his strength, solutions from crystals for protection from negative energy, and symbols of power carved into wood or painted with brightly colored dye on canvas are used as offerings in rituals or placed around your environment as reminders of light and beauty in dark times.

This chapter will explore Ogun's characteristics and traits, diving into the colors, chakras, animals, plants, crystals, symbols, and veves associated with him. It will also include information on what offerings and meals he prefers to receive. By understanding his energies and how to use them, you can appreciate the strength that Ogun offers you in greater depth. The more you understand Ogun, the better you can use his power in your everyday life.

Going Deeper into Ogun

In the Yoruba religion, Ogun is a symbol of strength and skill, represented not just by symbols but also colors, animals, and plants. The veve pattern is believed to be a way to direct energy in rituals to connect with the spirit of Ogun. Additionally, his red color often represents battle, leadership, and authority. It is believed that wearing red clothing during rituals helps to show respect for this complex Orisha.

The veve of Ogun (or Ogoun).
https://commons.wikimedia.org/wiki/File:VeveOgoun.svg

Ogun is also associated with animals, such as goats and dogs, which are said to have been his companions during trading journeys. These animals are sacrificed during celebrations in honor of Ogun. Lastly, many plants are seen as his companions, including melegueta pepper (grains of paradise), used for seasoning food, symbolic of opening the door for communication between oneself and the divine realm. So, through him, you can see how different symbols unite to honor this powerful deity. While these are just some of the symbols associated with

Ogun, it's worth diving deeper into the specifics and learning what they mean.

Ogun's Colors

Ogun is the Yoruba god of metalworking, war, and the hunt; he is represented in many cultures across the African continent. And if there's anything he's a master of, it's his signature red hues! Maroon, rust, and crimson are all divinely associated with Ogun; with them come power, authority, battle, and courage. Red is symbolic of the strength of this powerful deity. Red and all its dynamic tints and tones also signify the strength of will and spiritual power he gives his followers.

Ogun's Chakras

Ogun's primary chakra is powerfully associated with *the root chakra*, which symbolizes grounding and stability in difficult times. Those called to work with Ogun are guided by his presence and strength to stay rooted in their purpose during challenging moments of life. He helps you take action toward your goals, provides protection, facilitates courage and stability, and boosts creativity in problem-solving. Whether you are just learning about him or are an experienced devotee, you'll likely find comfort in his colorful chakra energy as he helps manage chaos with wisdom, balance, and strength.

Ogun is associated with the root chakra.
https://pixabay.com/es/illustrations/chakra-centros-energ%c3%a9ticos-cuerpo-3131630/

Ogun's Animal

Ogun is an incredibly powerful god, and it's no surprise that rams and roosters are associated with him. Rams represent strength and vitality in life, while roosters symbolize energetic positivity. In Yoruba culture, Ogun is honored through sacrificial offerings of these two animals to show reverence for his power. This connection between rams, roosters, and Ogun has been upheld since ancient times, a testament to God's importance within this cultural tradition.

Ogun's Plants

The mysterious and powerful Ogun has been associated with several plants and herbs, including melegueta pepper (grains of paradise). Not only is this herb very distinctively tasty in so many dishes, but it's also believed to open the doors of communication between the divine realm and oneself. Imagine what life could be like if you had direct access and understanding from the divine realm. Other plants associated with Ogun are agbo, calabash, and natal plums. The calabash tree is said to have been where Ogun first brewed his signature beverage of strength and courage, while the natal plums represent prosperity. Agbo is a Yoruba aphrodisiac, reinforcing Ogun's connection with fertility and creativity.

Ogun is associated with the melegueta pepper.

Adoscam, CC BY-SA 4.0 <https://creativecommons.org/licenses/by-sa/4.0>, via Wikimedia Commons https://commons.wikimedia.org/wiki/File:Graines_d%C3%A9cortiqu%C3%A9es_de_gousse_de_poivre_de_Guin%C3%A9e_ou_de_maniguette_ou_de_graine_de_paradis_ou_(ou_encore_atakoun_au_B%C3%A9nin).jpg

Ogun's Crystals

Ogun, the powerful Orisha of Nigeria and Benin, is associated with a few crystals that have certain unique benefits. Black tourmaline shields its holder from negative energy and provides strength and courage in difficult situations. Red jasper, a beautiful stone with a red tinge to it, restores balance and can bring peace amidst chaos. Lastly, the tiger's eye, and its seemingly endless depths, help you to understand yourself and create strong boundaries with the people around you. These powerful crystals associated with Ogun help promote positivity in your life.

Red jasper is one of the stones associated with Ogun, as it symbolizes restoring peace among chaos.
あおもりくま、 Aomorikuma, CC BY-SA 4.0 <https://creativecommons.org/licenses/by-sa/4.0>, via Wikimedia Commons
https://commons.wikimedia.org/wiki/File:Red_Jasper_Tugaru_Nishikiishi_Japan_IMG_8854.jpg

Ogun's Symbols

Ogun is known as a spirit of great strength, associated with both war and peace. As such, his symbols are diverse but also quite powerful. Ogun's symbols are made up of a machete, an axe, a chain or manacles, and a rum bottle or gin. All because these items represent the presence of strength that Ogun embodies. They indicate Ogun's capacity to unite multiple ideas and concepts into one powerful force. His overall power is often touted in many spiritual circles as being simply invincible!

While Ogun's symbols are powerful, they also represent a variety of meanings. Here is a breakdown of what each symbol stands for:

Ogun's Machete

A Machete is one of the most powerful symbols of Ogun, the god of iron in Yoruba mythology. It represents strength, power, and vitality that are essential for a successful life. Ogun is also believed to be the ancestor of blacksmiths who forged iron tools like machetes with skills and wisdom passed down from generation to generation. The machete was used not only for its practical uses, like clearing foliage during farming and harvesting crops, but also to indicate authority because of its power. The machete represents the strength and courage that come with an indomitable spirit and winning battles against adversity. It serves as a reminder that anything can be achieved through perseverance and discipline.

The machete represents courage and strength.
https://pixabay.com/es/photos/machete-tronco-naturaleza-campo-4528976/

Ogun's Axe

The Axe is an iconic symbol amongst many traditional African communities. It's associated with Ogun, the Yoruba warrior-creator God of Iron. The axe stands for courage and determination to grind through obstacles you may face in life. The symbolism of the tool reflects Ogun's ability to protect and guide his people. It also demonstrates that strength comes from persevering regardless of the situation. For many, an axe is a reminder to stay strong in hard times or when dealing with challenging situations. With the axe as a symbolic representation, followers are inspired to keep moving forward and achieve their goals despite any difficulties thrust upon them.

The axe represents the determination to push through any obstacle.
Brooklyn Museum, CC BY 3.0 <https://creativecommons.org/licenses/by/3.0>, via Wikimedia Commons
https://commons.wikimedia.org/wiki/File:Brooklyn_Museum_22.578_Axe_with_Handle_and_Blade.jpg

Ogun's Chain or Manacles

Ogun has long been associated with chains or manacles as symbols of his power to bind and control. While these objects can be seen as a form of restriction, they offer the promise of protection and strength when called on correctly. This can be seen in how Ogun's story is told across many parts of Africa. He saves warriors from enemies, helps craft tools for success, and forges paths for others to find freedom. Chains or manacles can also symbolize empowering the results that come from hard work and dedication, something befitting an ironworker like Ogun. At its core, this powerful symbol represents the strength that comes from facing challenges and staying committed!

Ogun's chain is a symbol of his ability to control and bind power.
https://unsplash.com/photos/2zGTh-S5moM

Rum Bottle or Gin

Ogun is often represented by a bottle of rum or gin. When these symbols are seen, they represent joy, celebration, and merrymaking. They also express strength and resiliency, both qualities that Ogun exemplifies and encourages in his worshipers. For many, these symbols are a reminder of Ogun's support and strength when times become difficult. Embracing these symbols is essential to honoring Ogun and the values he represents. Regardless of the situation, raising a toast with a glass of rum or gin reminds you that there can be joy in any circumstance.

The bottle represents celebration and joy.
https://www.pexels.com/photo/a-dark-brown-liquor-in-a-decanter-7253927/

Ogun's Veves

Ogun's veves are vibrant symbols found among a variety of African-based religions and cultures. These symbols typically include a cross and a circle inside which the figure of Ogun can be seen. Veves are used in spiritual ceremonies and signify an offering to Ogun, the spirit associated with strength, fertility, fire, and ironworking. He is both a protector of justice and capable of imparting good fortune. A veve then acts as an invocation to Ogun so that his energies may be summoned into existence and provide protection or blessing before beginning a ritual or undertaking an important task. Here's a deeper look into some of the most popular veves associated with Ogun.

- **The Veve of Earth:** This veve is represented by a small circle with a larger circle around it, symbolizing the cycle of death and renewal. This veve is used to invoke Ogun's protection and strength in times of difficulty or strife.
- The Veve of Water: This veve comprises two concentric circles, with an open eye in the middle. It is believed to offer protection from emotional and physical harm, as well as bring an abundance of luck and prosperity.
- The Veve of Fire: This symbol is often used to invoke Ogun's presence and power. It's formed by a circle with a triangle in the center, symbolizing Ogun's ability to bring transformation and protection. The triangle is also a reminder of Ogun's brave spirit.
- The Veve of Air: This veve is characterized by four circles connected in the center by a small line, symbolizing the four directions of the wind. This veve is used to invoke Ogun's wisdom and insight, as well as offer protection from harm.

Offerings and Meals for Ogun

Regarding offerings and meals for Ogun, the Yoruba people offer a wide variety of traditional meals and special items. Cooked food like jollof rice, roasted plantains, beef stews, and various other meals are regularly cooked to honor the spirit of Ogun. Additionally, items usually put out are fruits such as oranges, limes, and olives, together with other objects used in sacrifices such as candles, rum, and cigars. For more specific religious ceremonies involving Ogun, there are stronger offerings that include cocks and other animals sacrificed on his altar. These rituals involve prepared chants accompanied by special percussion instruments that reflect his presence as an Orisha or God in the Yoruba religion.

Here are some recipes which can be used to honor Ogun:

Jollof Rice

Ingredients:

- 2 cups of long-grain rice
- 2 tablespoons of vegetable oil
- 1 onion, finely chopped
- 2 cloves garlic, minced
- 1 teaspoon ginger, grated
- 1 teaspoon curry powder
- 1 teaspoon chili powder
- ½ teaspoon ground cumin
- 2 tablespoons tomato paste
- 2 cups chicken broth
- 1 can diced tomatoes
- Salt and pepper to taste

Instructions:

1. Heat oil in a large skillet over medium heat.
2. Add onions, garlic, ginger, and spices and cook until fragrant and the onions are translucent, about 5 minutes.
3. Add tomato paste and stir for 1 minute.
4. Add rice, chicken broth, and diced tomatoes, and season with salt and pepper.
5. Bring to a boil, reduce heat to low, and simmer covered for 20 minutes.
6. Remove the lid and fluff with a fork before serving.

Using this recipe to honor Ogun will bring good fortune and protection from harm. It can also be used in special religious ceremonies where Ogun is invoked to bring transformation and protection.

Roasted Plantains

Ingredients:
- 2 ripe plantains, sliced into 1-inch thick rounds
- 2 tablespoons olive oil
- Salt and pepper to taste

Instructions:
1. Preheat oven to 350°F.
2. Grease a baking sheet with olive oil.
3. Arrange the plantain slices in an even layer on the baking sheet.
4. Sprinkle with salt and pepper to taste.
5. Bake for 20 minutes, flipping halfway through until plantains are golden brown.

Serving roasted plantains as an offering to Ogun is a traditional way of honoring him and asking for protection and strength. Additionally, plantains are believed to bring good luck and prosperity in times of difficulty or strife.

Beef Stew

Ingredients:
- 2 tablespoons vegetable oil
- 1 onion, diced
- 1 pound beef stew meat, cubed
- 2 cloves garlic, minced
- 2 carrots, peeled and diced
- 1 celery stalk, diced
- 1 teaspoon ground cumin
- 1 teaspoon paprika
- ½ teaspoon dried oregano
- 2 tablespoons tomato paste
- 2 cups beef broth
- 2 cups potatoes, diced

- Salt and pepper to taste

Instructions:
1. Heat oil in a large skillet over medium heat.
2. Add onions and beef and cook until lightly browned, 8-10 minutes.
3. Add garlic, carrots, and celery, and cook for an additional 5 minutes.
4. Add cumin, paprika, oregano, and tomato paste and stir to coat the beef and vegetables.
5. Add the beef broth and potatoes and bring to a boil.
6. Cover, reduce heat to low, and simmer for 1 hour.
7. Remove the lid and season with salt and pepper before serving.

Serving a beef stew around a sacred fire is believed to show respect to Ogun and can bring positive energy in the form of protection, strength, and courage. The beef stew is a symbol of sustenance and nourishment, which are important elements when honoring Ogun.

Ogun is a hugely influential and powerful deity in the Yoruba religion. He is associated with strength, courage, and protection from harm. Symbols such as a machete, hammer, and veves can be used to call down his spirit and bring positive energy. His colors are red, black, and blue, his chakra is the first or root chakra, his animal is a ram, and his plant is cotton. His crystal is jasper, and his symbols are the machete, hammer, and veves. He is often called down with a specific veve, believed to bring forth his spirit and protection. Offering him rum, cigars, incense, and traditional meals such as beef stew or roasted plantains is a good way to honor him.

Furthermore, Ogun likes to receive a variety of foods and drinks as offerings, including rum, cigars, and traditional meals such as beef stew or roasted plantains. Eating these meals can bring good fortune and protection from harm – while invoking Ogun through symbols and veves can bring transformation and protection. Therefore, by honoring Ogun in these ways, one can bring positive energy into their life.

Chapter 7: Making a Sacred Altar

Dedicating a shrine to Ogun can be an awesome experience full of significance and an invaluable way to honor the Orisha. Not only is it beautiful and captivating to create a space that captures your vibrant interpretations of Ogun, but it also serves to deepen and enrich your spiritual journey with him. A creative offering of visual expressions, such as art pieces and even scents, can be put together in a way that makes you feel deeply connected with Ogun. With time and practice, shrines can become powerful spiritual tools used to petition Ogun's guidance, protection, strength, and blessings on your life.

Ogun altar.
https://commons.wikimedia.org/wiki/File:Acentamento_de_Ogum,_Orossi.,JPG

This chapter discusses the benefits of building a shrine to Ogun, where to create it, what to place on it and how to take care of it, how to give offerings through it, and when to clear the gifts. It will also provide examples of traditional shrines and offerings. By the end of this chapter, you'll have a better understanding of how to create and maintain your own Ogun altar. The knowledge shared here will help you to make your spiritual journey with Ogun more meaningful and powerful.

Benefits of Building a Shrine to Ogun

The African deity Ogun brings immense good fortune and strength to those who worship him. Building a shrine can be an excellent way to honor Ogun and take advantage of the blessings he bestows on those who pay tribute to him. According to legend, having a shrine can protect against misfortune, promote prosperity, and even create opportunities for advancement. It can also serve as a reminder of one's spiritual beliefs and keep them close to the heart, especially in difficult times. It also offers a central location for rituals or ceremonies held in honor of Ogun, ensuring his legendary power remains ever-present. Ultimately, building a shrine to Ogun is a powerful spiritual practice that not only honors the deity but could potentially lead an individual or community toward the path of success.

A. Respecting and Honoring Ogun

Building a shrine to honor and respect Ogun can bring immense blessings into your life. Not only will you be in Oguns' favor and protected by his presence, but you may also find yourself gifted with increased creativity, freedom of expression, and enriched physical well-being. By creating an altar or shrine dedicated to Ogun, you are inviting his potent energies into your life and allowing him to bring abundance to new areas of your existence. Showing reverence, respect, and care for this great deity can lead to blessings far greater than you could ever imagine!

B. Strengthening the Connection with Ogun

Building a shrine to Ogun is said to be the best way to strengthen your connection with this powerful and respected Orisha. Adding an altar in your home or community serves as an essential reminder of his blessings and helps create a spiritual atmosphere in which to receive divine guidance. Regular sacrifices and offerings at the shrine will generate positive manifestations such as improved health, enhanced focus and productivity, increased wealth and prosperity, and secure protection from enemies, both seen and unseen. As your connection deepens over time with Ogun, through contemplation and reverence before the altar, you may experience an even more profound transformation within yourself.

C. A Place of Emotional Support and Comfort

Building a shrine to Ogun bring with it many benefits, and one of the most significant is providing emotional support and comfort. By gathering with other followers to honor and celebrate Ogun, participants experience a sense of connection that can help reduce feelings of isolation. Offerings made at these shrines are also a great source of solace. For example, small items such as food or drink are given in appreciation for Ogun's guidance, providing physical nourishment and spiritual renewal. Ultimately, when you take time to unite and venerate, your actions will positively strengthen you emotionally and spiritually.

D. A Place for Ogun to Grant Blessings

Building a shrine to Ogun comes with so many benefits and can be a great way to practice your faith. As a sacred place to come to pray and bask in the presence of the gods, it's also an opportunity to experience the prosperity and peace that Ogun can grant an individual. When you place your faith in Ogun, this deity provides safety and protection, financial security, and general guidance throughout everyday life. Furthermore, having a designated place to recharge spiritually from daily stress brings more balance into your life, leaving you more energized and motivated. A shrine to Ogun is good for individuals and families wishing to keep the ancient traditions alive, blessing themselves with strong community support. With all these amazing benefits, building a shrine to Ogun is worth every second of the time and effort you put into it.

E. A Place to Share Blessings with Others

Building a shrine to the Yoruba god Ogun is a meaningful and interesting way to share blessings with others. It's an incredibly powerful way to connect with the energetic forces of Orisha and tap into his potential to help improve your life and the lives of those around you. It's also a great way to honor Ogun and embrace his attributes, such as knowledge, innovation, courage, strength, protection, and more.

Building a shrine embodying these core values is honoring Ogun and reminding yourself why he is necessary to your spiritual journey. And for those who have already established a connection with the Orisha, it's an opportunity to show devotion in a tangible form through artwork or decoration on the shrine. By creating this sacred space dedicated to him and sharing joy with others, you can ensure your blessings are being passed along in an abundant flow.

Where to Create an Ogun Altar

Ogun is an important deity in many African traditions, and having a personal altar dedicated to him is a deeply spiritual veneration of this powerful god. When creating an Ogun altar, it is critical to think carefully about how and where to set it up. An ideal place for such an altar would be somewhere outdoors, like a backyard or natural area that feels connected to the Earth. This will help you feel at one with the environment, much like the spirit of Ogun.

However, sometimes it's not feasible or convenient for everyone to have an outdoor altar. In these cases, setting up your altar indoors can also be meaningful if done thoughtfully. The key is finding a comfortable and private space to focus on worshipping Ogun without any distractions. Ultimately, you should create a space that reflects your relationship with Ogun and makes you feel connected to him on a deeper level.

A. Indoors or Outdoors

When it comes to creating an Ogun altar, the choice between indoors and outdoors can be difficult. While an outdoor altar is sure to capture attention and create an impressive sight, some worries about safety and security may become an issue. An indoor alternative may provide more privacy but require a more creative and thoughtful setup. Before picking a location for your altar, consider both options carefully so that you can create the atmosphere you want, whether it be mystical and comforting or awe-inspiring and powerful. Ultimately, the decision of where you choose to create your Ogun altar should depend on what works best for your goals.

B. Location and Direction

When creating an Ogun altar, it is vital to choose the right location. Ogun's power lies in the depths of metals, and it is believed that his altars should be mounted on an open rock in a public area. An ideal location would be a mountaintop or a crossroads, as these areas are symbols of transformation and justice, which are also principles deeply rooted within this tradition. This ensures that you are aligning yourself with the energies of Ogun while allowing it to reach its full potential, bringing strength, perception, and determination into your life.

C. Size and Design of the Shrine

When creating an Ogun altar, think carefully about size and design. If the space is large, the larger the shrine can be and more elaborate in terms of decorations. But a modest altar can still attract positive energy if only a smaller area is available. When selecting adornments or materials for the altar, choose items that speak to your spirituality as well as Ogun's principles. These can be anything from beads and fabric to feathers or jewelry. Consider your color scheme carefully. Most altars use red, black, and white with touches of green or blue to represent the four cardinal directions. Above all else, when choosing where to create an Ogun altar, ensure it is a spot where you feel comfortable and safe. Its purpose is to energize you spiritually and connect you with this powerful deity!

What to Place on an Ogun Altar

Making an altar to Ogun is a great way to honor and show your devotion to the Yoruba deity. Though many materials can be placed on an Ogun altar, some of the most common include wooden and metal elements, such as knives or axes, which symbolize his power over iron tools. You'll also want to add drinking and cooking items, like a pot or traditional gourd cleaners or "Osun," which symbolize his help with cooking up delicious food for the family.

Red cloth is also commonly used since it is intended as a reminder of Ogun's ability to break through any obstacle and clear the way ahead. Finally, you should consider adding stones from around your home or nearby riverbeds since nature-based elements have always been important in African religions. With these meaningful additions to your altar, you can demonstrate your appreciation for Ogun's role in the spiritual world!

A. Traditional Offerings

The Ogun altar is a sacred space honoring the Yoruba Orisha, Ogun. It is traditional to leave offerings on the altar to honor and give respect to the Orisha, who is known as the patron of technology, blacksmiths, war, and hunting. Common offerings include cowrie shells, red and white cloths, kola nuts, palm oil, yams or potatoes, coins, rum or gin, cigars, or cigarettes. In addition to these offerings, it's also customary for devotees of Ogun to create items for his altar that are built out of metal, such as scissors and other tools which can symbolically connect him with our creative and technological endeavors. By leaving items on his altar that are meaningful to you, you aim to reaffirm your relationship with the spirit realm and honor your connection with the divine through honoring Ogun.

B. Symbols of Protection and Strength

Ogun altars are a great way to embrace the power and protection of the Ogun spirit. To create an altar, start by gathering symbolic items connected to strength and safety. Some good choices could include a bright red piece of fabric or cloth, useful tools such as hammers and tongs for demonstration of strength or protection, dried or fresh herbs which visually evoke protection like rosemary, salt for cleansing and protection against evil, stones or shells for grounding energy, candles to lead the way, incense-like camphor, or copal to purify the space and enhance your spiritual connection with Ogun, and perhaps an image of Ogun himself. With each item placed on the altar, ask Ogun to infuse it with his energy. Focusing on your intentions can help you enjoy the power of your altar to its fullest extent.

C. A Statue of Ogun

Ogun, the Yoruba Orisha of iron and war, is honored with a statue or altar. Whether you are a Yoruba devotee of Ogun or greatly appreciate Yoruba culture, creating an Ogun altar can be a wonderful way to pay tribute to this powerful deity. An altar should include things such as stones, coins, dried herbs, and leaves from plants representing protection and prosperity, like Olugbo leaf and bitter kola, vegetable oils for illumination, prayer beads and bells for spiritual cleansing, and brass tools representing power. If you already have an Ogun statue, candles could be lit in front of it as expressions of respect and as an offering of thanks. Whatever objects are included on your altar will be unique to your connection to the Orisha deity honoring him in all his glory.

D. Candles

If you are making or setting up an altar to the Orisha Ogun, you may be wondering what candles to use. Candles are a simple but powerful way to call upon and pay tribute to this powerful God of iron and forge. Consider black, red, and white candles for your altar when working with Ogun's energy. Black candles are great for protection and material success, red for joy, strength, vitality, and power, and white for devotion and spiritual growth. You can also combine all three colors in one large candle or place them side-by-side around your altar. Adding coins from different countries is another powerful way to show appreciation to Ogun, as coins represent wealth in all forms, such as currency, knowledge, and wealth of energy. Lastly, adding an offering of assorted fresh fruit (such as apples or oranges) or a strong drink, such as a glass of whisky, on top of the altar will please him greatly, ensuring his blessings are reaped again and again.

E. Incense and Other Scents

Incense and other scents are also great for setting the atmosphere around an Ogun altar. Ogun is known as the warrior of change, so many people use this deity to honor their bravery and transition in life. Incense is often used on an Ogun altar because it is believed to open up portals between worlds, enabling communication between humans and spirits. People may also consider placing aromatic herbs like Hops, Rosemary, Vervain, Angelica root, and Sarsaparilla as offerings in their Ogun altar. Each herb has its own special properties that work together with the energies within nature or even within yourself to create powerful changes. Heavily scented oils such as sandalwood or patchouli can also be used to help bring good luck and success during times of upheaval or transition.

How to Take Care of the Altar

Taking care of your altar is essential to honoring and connecting with this beloved spirit. We suggest you regularly give offerings and sacrifices on your altar to show respect and gratitude, especially when you have asked for specific things from the deity. You should also cleanse your shrine around once a week by burning incense; you might try a leathery scent used traditionally in Orisha worship. Make sure the altar is well-lit and free from any clutter or dust. Filling it with fresh fruit, flowers, or other natural offerings is a great idea too! Overall, taking care of an Ogun altar requires consistent commitment, but the rewards in your spiritual experience can be immeasurable.

How to Give Offerings through an Ogun Altar

Ogun, who is one of the oldest deities in Yoruba mythology, can be honored at an altar with offerings. It's a great way to show your respect for Ogun and maintain a connection with him. To make your offering, start by cleaning your hands and preparing the space where you intend to honor Ogun. Make sure it is neat and inviting so that you can focus on offering your reverence. Then, choose a gift appropriate to the occasion and align it with Ogun's values. Think along the lines of farm tools, machetes, or any type of iron items for strength. Place these in front of the altar as if welcoming him into your home and express gratitude for his presence in your life. Finally, spend some time in meditation before dispersing energies with gratitude and light humming sounds. This is a great way to establish a strong relationship with Ogun's energy!

When to Clear Offerings from an Ogun Altar

Clearing offerings from an Ogun altar is an important practice for anyone honoring the deity. The methods used to clear these offerings depend on individual preference and may range from physical disposal and/or burning of offerings. The frequency of clearing should respond to signs that appear when it is time to remove offerings, such as shifts in energy or feelings of heaviness. Reaching out and paying attention to the spirit realm can provide clues that it is time to clear the altar and ensure your Ogun altar is regularly refreshed with the intention and presence of honor, respect, and adoration.

Examples of Ogun Shrines and Offerings

Ogun, the Yoruba god of iron and war, is honored with shrines throughout Africa and countries in the African diaspora. The celebration varies from region to region, but all celebrations involve offerings placed at the shrine. Depending on the area, these offerings can include the sacrifice of chickens or goats, palming coins, pouring libations of palm wine or rum, burning paper money or items symbolic of Ogun's power, and iron tools such as machetes, hatchets, and hoes, and by leaving alcohol for him to drink. More modern forms of celebrating Ogun include cultural performances such as drumming, dancing, and singing songs dedicated to him. All of these offerings are made with the understanding that although Ogun can be a destructive force when he needs to be in wartime, he is also generous to his followers, who honor him faithfully with devotion.

Honoring Ogun with an altar is a great way to connect and show your appreciation for this powerful spirit. Creating an altar involves setting up a clean and inviting space, offering items or sacrifices specific to Ogun's values, and regularly clearing away these offerings. With consistent commitment and effort, connecting to Ogun through an altar can be a rewarding part of your spiritual practice. It is also vital to remember that although Ogun can be a destructive force in wartime, when necessary, he is also generous to his followers, who honor him faithfully. One way of showing your respect is by connecting to Ogun through an altar, offering appropriate items and sacrifices, regularly clearing these away as instructed, and always showing sincere devotion. A connection and relationship with Ogun can be achieved with dedication and effort.

Chapter 8: Useful Rituals and Spells

Ogun, the highly respected warrior spirit, can bestow great power of protection, strength, and clarity on his followers. His presence increases your self-confidence by guiding you through paths of obstacles and conflict and helping elicit creative solutions to problems, increase productivity, help with troubleshooting, and overcome blocks. His presence also guides physical traveling or journeying on a spiritual level. By completing rituals or offerings for Ogun, you open yourself up to receive his blessings in these areas. All it takes is an open heart, faith, and trust for him to come and guide you whenever you need it.

This chapter outlines recipes for spells, rituals, and prayers dedicated to Ogun. All the necessary ingredients are listed with steps to take for protection, self-confidence, creativity, productivity, and traveling. By following these with reverence, respect, and mindfulness, you can invoke the power of Ogun to help manifest your intentions. Remember that any spell or ritual should be done with a clear and pure intention, as Ogun's power can be destructive and productive depending on one's intention.

Protection

Ogun, also known as the Dauntless Warrior and Master of Iron, is an influential deity in the Yoruba pantheon. Those looking for protection can find strength and guidance through rituals, spells, and offerings to Ogun. Many of these offer recognition and respect to this great god while helping proprietors build a spiritual connection with him. Inciting Ogun's protection can be done through ancestral offerings such as animal sacrifices or honey libations. Other protective symbols, such as iron nails or four-pointed stars, are also appreciated by Ogun.

Spells invoking Ogun tend to involve singing, dancing, drums, and sharing stories of courage and bravery, the qualities held in high esteem by the deity himself. In addition to speaking prayers of protection in the direction of an iron shrine dedicated to Ogun, other rituals like meditation are also useful for reaching out to the Dauntless Warrior for help. Of course, not all fear can be blocked with spells or formulas. Sometimes courage has to come from within, and with a little help from your deities, you'll find a path through any darkness.

Ritual to Protect Your Home from Unwanted Influences

Creating a safe, peaceful home can be tricky. Ogun is an incredibly powerful energy we can call on when we're looking for extra protection. From simple sprinkling of salt and bay leaves to offerings and more involved rituals, there are also plenty of spells using Ogun's energy to protect your home from outside influences. Whether you are looking for his power to guard your physical dwelling or metaphorical home against darkness, the strength of Ogun gives us the potential to keep our cherished places of peace safe for ourselves and those we love.

The Sprinkle Salt and Bay Leaves ritual requires only a few ingredients and is effective for many kinds of protection. Here's a detailed recipe:

Ingredients:
- 1 white candle
- 1 black candle
- 2 tablespoons of sandalwood incense
- Salt
- Bay leaves

Instructions:
1. Start by creating a sacred space in your home by lighting the white candle and the black candle.

2. Chant a prayer or invocation to Ogun and ask for protection from all that is negative, unwanted, and harmful.
3. Take the salt and bay leaves in your hands and sprinkle them around the perimeter of your home, starting at the front door. Visualize a protective barrier surrounding your home to give you strength and courage.
4. Finally, light the sandalwood incense and walk around the house, allowing the smoke to purify and cleanse all rooms.
5. Allow the candles to burn out naturally, and use this time for meditation and reflection on the protection that Ogun brings.

Ritual for Protection against Negative Thought Patterns

Practicing rituals to protect against negative thoughts establishes healthy practices that balance our mental health and well-being. Ogun, the Yoruba spirit of iron, is one powerful figure who many turn to for protection from negative thoughts or unwanted energies. There are a variety of useful chants, invocations, and spells related to Ogun, which can be used depending on what you need. Grounding meditations and visualization exercises can further empower a person seeking protection from negative mental cycles. Connecting with the strength of Ogun through these practices can help you find greater resilience in times of difficulty and trust in your innate power.

Rituals to Combat Bullying

Ogun embodies strength, craftsmanship, and war and is an important figure in many rituals. If you've experienced bullying or know someone who has, Ogun can provide powerful protection. Incorporating Ogun into your rituals to combat bullying could bring about comfort and a sense of security. He can provide the timely boost of courage and assurance that, so often, what is needed in the face of bullying. With his protection, you can find resilience no matter the situation. In ceremonies involving Ogun, powerful trinkets such as iron, black textile, honeycomb, and healing stones are used as offerings to invoke his presence. These meaningful rituals could be especially beneficial to those who have gone through extreme bouts of bullying, providing solace where none seemed possible before.

Self-Confidence

Ogun is connected to many different skills and passions. One of these is self-confidence, which can be built through a variety of different rituals and spells. Ogun's powerful spirit can help you grow and develop your self-assurance through certain offerings and recitations. However, remember that you are the main driver of your self-confidence. All Ogun can do is provide an extra bit of support on your journey toward feeling comfortable in your skin.

Spells and Rituals to Help with Low Self-Esteem

One of the most empowering practices for anyone struggling with low self-esteem is to turn to Ogun. Spells and rituals devoted to him can be immensely helpful in helping you reclaim your true identity and power. The aim is to fill yourself with courage, strength, and resilience to bravely confront any obstacles life may bring.

When you feel unworthy or defenseless against life's difficulties, calling on Ogun can provide courage through his strong nature. Similarly, symbols related to Ogun can be used as reminders of strength and be placed around the home as talismans of security. Through spell casting, offerings, and daily affirmations, you may find yourself becoming more vibrant in both the physical and spiritual spaces. By strengthening yourself internally, facing your fears or anxieties head-on may become easier so that paths to empowerment can truly start leading you down a new path.

Spell work to Boost Self-Confidence and Courage

Ogun is the traditional Orisha of strength and courage, providing faith and protection to African people for centuries. He is undoubtedly a powerful ally, especially when it comes to modern-day struggles with self-confidence, fear, and anxiety. If you're looking to gently remove obstacles, reaching out to Ogun may be just the thing you need.

Whether through ritual or spell work, Ogun can help guide you on the path toward new levels of self-acceptance and fearlessness. Amongst other activities, such as creating affirmations or speaking incantations relevant to your goals, one basic ritual is as follows:

Ingredients:
- Honeycomb
- Iron trinkets/nails/rings
- Candles (preferably black or blue)
- Stones of your choice

Instructions:
1. Place the iron trinkets, honeycomb, and stones on an altar or any other sacred space of your choice.
2. Light the candles, and begin to focus all of your energy on the items in front of you.
3. Speak out loud your intention for the spell, or recite a prayer or incantation dedicated to Ogun (see below for one example).
4. Leave the items and candles on the altar until they have burned out, then discard them safely and respectfully.

Prayer to Ogun

"Ogun, sacred spirit of strength, courage, and power, I ask you to grant me divine protection so that I may have the strength and courage to face my fears. Fill me with infinite peace, clarity, and understanding so that I may be free from worry and anxiety. Protect me from the forces of darkness, and guide me to new heights of self-confidence and power. I offer my humble gratitude and devotion at this moment. May it be returned tenfold. Amen."

Once the spell is completed, and the prayer said, keep your energies high by following up with affirmations or activities that help you stay focused on your goals. With Ogun's help, the path to self-empowerment should become clearer and more attainable.

Meditations for Overcoming Fear

When it comes to overcoming fear, there might not be a better tool than Ogun. He is a powerful protector and warrior who comes to the aid of those who need it most. Through meditations and rituals in the Yoruba tradition, you can tap into the power of Ogun to help you move through fear and into courage and action. There are a wide variety of rituals for accessing Ogun's help, depending on what you need, from personal protection spells to rituals for banishing anxiety. Whether you're feeling overwhelmed or looking for an empowering boost, connecting with Ogun can be an invaluable resource on your journey toward conquering your fears.

Here are a few exercises to consider:

- Visualize yourself facing and conquering your fears by calling on Ogun's power. Imagine his fiery energy providing you with strength, protection, and courage.
- Recite a prayer or incantation to Ogun that reflects your current goals (see above for an example).
- Create a physical altar or offering to Ogun with items of your choosing.
- Engage in active visualization. Imagine a protective shield around yourself, empowered by Ogun's energy.
- Participate in meditation-focused rituals such as "shaking out" negative energy (this involves physically shaking your body as if you are shaking out old, stagnant energy).
- Spend time in nature and take a moment to appreciate the power of Ogun and the protective energy he provides.

Creativity

Ogun is a powerful spirit associated with creativity and transformation, particularly relating to new beginnings. Many wonderful rituals and spells are available to honor this spirit to embody his transformative energy in your life. One popular practice that helps to unleash creativity is ancestor reverence which means relating stories of your ancestors, honoring them through offerings such as candles or fruit, and weaving their lessons into your life.

Incorporating drumming or chants related to Ogun can also create a much-needed path for creative flow while allowing you to connect deeply with this powerful force. Whatever ritual you choose, remembering to be mindful of the vibrant energy it brings to your creative endeavors can make all the difference in unlocking Ogun's transformative power within you!

Rituals to Unblock Creativity

There are many rituals and spells to unleash creativity that involve calling upon the energy of Ogun. When beginning a creative process, it can be helpful to call on Ogun's energy asking for guidance to overcome any blocks or inhibitions. Here are a few rituals to reignite the creative process:

- **Burning Offerings** - Light a candle or incense to symbolize your offering of gratitude and respect to Ogun.
- **Drumming** - Use a drum or other percussion instrument to create energy and open up the creative path.
- **Dancing** - Find a rhythm and allow yourself to move freely as you invoke Ogun's energy.
- **Prayer** - Recite a prayer or chant to Ogun, expressing your gratitude and asking for guidance in overcoming creative blocks.
- **Ancestor Veneration** - Spend time in conversation or offer an offering to your ancestors and ask for their guidance on your creative path.
- **Nature walks** - Spend time in nature, reflecting on the power of Ogun and asking for guidance.

Ritual for Abundance and Opportunity

Ogun can also be a powerful ally to manifest abundance and create opportunities for success. When working with Ogun's energy, it can be helpful to focus on taking action, as his energy is associated with assertive force and strength. Here are rituals to help bring abundance and opportunity into your life:

Ingredients:
- White or brown candle
- Seven coins (or another offering to Ogun)
- Fire-safe container

Steps:
1. Place the candle in your fire-safe container and light it.
2. Call upon Ogun, asking for his assistance in manifesting abundance and creating opportunities for success.

3. Place the coins in a circle around the candle.
4. Visualize the energy of abundance and opportunity radiating out from the candle in a circular pattern.
5. Speak your intentions aloud for what you want to attract into your life.
6. When finished, allow the candle to burn out safely in the fire-safe container.
7. Offer your gratitude to Ogun for his assistance.

You can also connect with Ogun's energy by reciting this prayer:

"Ogun, mighty warrior and protector, I come to you seeking your guidance. Help me to forge a path of abundance and opportunity. Help me to be brave in the pursuit of my goals. I thank you for your strength and protection on my journey."

By using these rituals and prayers, you can draw upon Ogun's energy to help manifest abundance and create opportunities for success in your life.

Cleansing Ritual

Ogun's energy can be used to cleanse and clear away any obstacles in your life, opening up avenues for new possibilities and beginnings. Practicing rituals or ceremonies involving taking advantage of Ogun's energy can be beneficial, such as lighting candles to help you meditate and focus on his power. As you tap into his strengths, they can become your own, helping to clear out any negative feelings or clutter that may have been blocking the way forward. Once freed from these restrictions, you'll find yourself more open than ever before to new opportunities and possibilities.

Here is a cleansing ritual that can be used to clear the way for new beginnings:

Ingredients:
- White candle
- Garlic
- Frankincense
- A bowl of water
- Salt

Steps:
1. Begin by carving your name into the candle. Place the garlic and frankincense around the candle.
2. Light the candle and pray to Ogun for protection, cleansing, and any new opportunities you wish to manifest in your life.
3. Sprinkle a pinch of salt into the bowl of water and stir with your fingers as you focus on your intent for the ritual.
4. Dip your fingers into the water and sprinkle it around the room you're in as an offering to Ogun.
5. Allow the candle to burn completely, and give thanks to Ogun for his guidance and protection.

Ogun Prayer:

"Ogun, Ogun. I ask for protection, cleansing, and blessings upon me. Guide me through my journey and open the paths that are meant for me. I thank you for your blessings and trust in your divine guidance. Amen."

For centuries, Ogun has been revered for his power and strength. He is still a great source of protection, cleansing, and the opening of paths for those who seek it. Through the use of rituals and prayers, Ogun helps people manifest their desires into reality. This chapter has outlined some rituals and prayers that can be used to draw on Ogun's energy and help bring abundance, opportunity, protection, and cleansing into your life. May you find success in all of your endeavors with his blessings!

Chapter 9: Ogun's Festivals and Holy Days

Each year, the Yoruba people of Nigeria and other West African countries celebrate the Ogun festival with joy and exuberance, honoring Ogun. He is a powerful archetype revered for his enduring strength in navigating challenging circumstances, qualities the Yoruba people continue to embody today. The celebration itself lasts for days, at times featuring parades and sacrifices in addition to performances from religious dance troupes.

Many West African countries celebrate the Ogun festival every year.
South African Tourism from South Africa, CC BY 2.0
<https://creativecommons.org/licenses/by/2.0>, via Wikimedia Commons
https://commons.wikimedia.org/wiki/File:Zulu_Culture,_KwaZulu-Natal,_South_Africa_(20325264550).jpg

While the rituals may differ across different regions, it's certain that wherever it's celebrated, Ogun's festival serves as an integral part of cultures that have survived and grown through time and never lost sight of the traditions that underpin them. This chapter explores the origins of Ogun's festival, how it's celebrated today, and why, as well as tips for honoring the deity in our daily lives. The chapter also dives into Ogun's feast day (which coincides with Saint Peter's Day) and the days associated with Ogun to provide a holistic overview of this important festival and its relevance in modern-day Yoruba culture.

Ogun's Festival

This traditional Yoruba festival honors Ogun, the god of iron and war. Thousands of devotees congregate to pray, sing, dance, and make offerings to show their reverence for Ogun's power and strength. Celebrations can last anywhere from three days to several weeks and are held to honor Ogun and all the gods associated with him. Daytime activities consist of parades featuring colorful costumes and ornately decorated pieces made from metal and iron, including swords and farm tools. In the evening, there are sacred ceremonies of prayers, music, and special meals created using ingredients believed to bring God's blessings. If you have a chance to witness or participate in such an event firsthand, don't hesitate, it will be a memorable experience!

Origins of the Festival

Ogun's festival is an annual celebration held in Nigeria and other West African countries. Its origin dates far back in ancient history when warriors used iron on their weapons for protection. Ogun was thought to be so powerful that an entire festival was created in his honor. Every year thousands of attendees gather to participate in rituals that include drumming and dancing, believed to be a grand show of respect for Ogun's strength and power. People dress up in traditional clothing and enjoy a variety of food made especially for a holiday. Ogun's Festival continues to live on today in traditional societies that want to pay tribute to their ancestral roots by honoring this remarkable deity.

Celebrations and Rituals

Ogun's Festival, also known as Oguinha, is a spectacular and vibrant celebration of the Yoruba religion. Colorful costumes, elaborate masquerade dances, drumming music, and lively parades fill the streets to honor Ogun by offering ceremonies at sacred sites. Families come together to share traditional dishes and exchange blessings while worshiping Ogun. This special period allows families to strengthen the bonds in their relationships and appreciate each other on a much deeper level. The energy of this joyous event is truly infectious. Even those who are not religious can join in on the festivities as long as they respect the culture's customs.

Ogun's Pilgrimage

Ogun's Pilgrimage is an annual celebration of the Yoruba god of iron, metallurgy, and hunting in parts of southwestern Nigeria. This spiritual pilgrimage has been traditionally celebrated for centuries and continues to be celebrated today. Every year, people dress in all-white garments to symbolize spiritual purity and ritual cleanliness. Led by senior members of Ogun, devotees march around the sacred space dedicated to Ogun to access blessings.

During this time, beautiful displays of vibrant energy accompanied by instrumental music and rhythmic dancing bring celebrations alive. There are also traditional offerings made in honor of Ogun, such as kola nuts and palm wine presented by devotees honoring Ogun's power over growth and sustenance, which he provides. This historical event is alive with energy and devotion as Yoruba people come together to seek spiritual guidance from their beloved Ogun. It's truly an awesome experience worth seeing if you get given the opportunity.

Feasting and Dancing

Celebrated from August through September, Ogun's Festival is known for its feasting and dancing. Feasting and large communal meals are shared among community members and speak to the importance of social bonds in Yoruba culture. Additionally, energetic dancing is a mainstay of the celebrations. It engages and energizes community members, showcasing their creativity and rich culture. All festival attendees dress in their finery as they come together to honor Ogun while engaging with one another. The colorful costumes and lively music create a vibrant atmosphere.

Processions and Parades

Each year, processions and parades are held where community members carry colorful umbrellas along with implements made of iron, such as spears or tools used to cut metal, while they march around various parts of Yoruba land. It is a ritualistic tradition with inspirational, joyous music, culminating in a grand feast given by the host village. It doesn't matter where you are from. If you're looking for an exciting cultural experience, be sure to get out to participate in these boisterous festivals!

Contemporary Significance in Yoruba Culture

To this day, this festival remains an important date in the Yoruba cultural calendar. Traditionally, it is acknowledged through rituals, feasting, and offering sacrifices. Nowadays, the festival embodies Yoruba values that transcend societal structures, focusing on justice, equal access to opportunities, and collective progress. It provides an opportunity for family members and friends to come together as one to live life in balance.

Ogun's Festival reinforces our shared understanding that we should continue to move forward as a collective, both spiritually and economically. This shared value system reinforces beliefs about accountability for positive communal action at the end of each season's festival period. People pray for another year filled with an increased understanding of the world and treasure what it means to live as stewards of this beautiful earth as our ancestors intended.

How to Celebrate Ogun's Festival

The Ogun Festival is such an exciting time, and there are so many ways that people can come together to celebrate it. Taking part in traditional ceremonies is one way to honor the spirit of Ogun. The festival is a time of joyous celebration, filled with the sounds of laughter and merriment. So having a parade around your community with drums, flutes, and whatever instruments you can get your hands on would be sure to make an impression. If you're looking for a more mellow approach, cooking up some tasty dishes like cassava bread or plantain pottage are all fun ways to celebrate. And don't forget that part of Ogun's strength and power comes from being able to help others; making donations to a local charity or offering assistance in some form would also be an excellent way to pay homage this season. Have fun celebrating!

Ogun's Feast Day

Ogun's Feast Day is a celebration of the fearsome god from Yoruban mythology, who is the leader of all warriors. By honoring him on his feast day, devotees pray for protection and hope for their enemies to be vanquished. In most celebrations, offerings traditionally consist of food, drink, and drums. As people gather together to mark this special day, it's also an opportunity to connect and continue to share stories of Ogun's heroic deeds while enjoying the company of family and friends. The reverence of Ogun is intended to unite all people rather than divide them, making his feast day a beautiful reminder that no matter our differences, we still have much in common.

When Is It Celebrated?

Ogun's Feast Day is a much-anticipated celebration for the Yoruba people every year. Taking place over three days, starting from the first to the third day of the fourth month of their calendar. People participate in many cultural activities and traditional prayers as they thank Ogun, their god of iron and technology. Activities may include singing, dancing, and feasting exquisite delicacies prepared specially for the festival. As well as being an important spiritual event in honor of Ogun, the feast day is also a great opportunity for families and friends to come together in celebration.

Celebrations in Different Regions

Across West Africa, members of the Yoruba diaspora gather to honor Ogun and show their appreciation for his protection. An intricately planned ceremony featuring music, singing, dancing, and unique local dishes is the climax of a month-long celebration. During this time of gratitude, celebrants donate money to those in need and distribute food to honor Ogun's generosity. Participants in the festival often leave offerings at shrines that are erected during the event to thank their deities for protecting them from harm over the past year. All who take part leave feeling inspired by Ogun's graciousness, forming memories that last far beyond the festival's end.

Offerings and Activities

During this annual celebration, all kinds of offerings and activities take place in honor of Ogun, from homemade metal implements to sacrificing animals. Many people also enjoy taking part in drum circles, feasts featuring traditional Nigerian dishes, and lively dancing from different parts of the country. Everyone is welcome to join the festivities or simply observe as they happen. However you choose to participate, Ogun's feast day is sure to be an amazing experience!

Days Associated with Ogun

Ogun, an ancient god of the Yoruba pantheon, represents virility and power. He is strong and brave, able to forge his path. This spirit of strength and determination is why many cultures across the continent honor Ogun on special days. Tuesdays are especially associated with him, as they are seen as days of courage and strength that break through any obstacles encountered in a person's journey. Wednesdays also represent Ogun's steadiness and resilience, a day named to remind you that you can hold firm to your dreams regardless of what life throws your way. Lastly, Ogun is honored on the fourth day of every month. This special remembrance serves as an opportunity to reflect on the past and call on his energy so that you can strive for greatness in your present endeavors. Celebrations dedicated to Ogun remind everyone to remain determined in pursuit of their goals!

How to Honor Ogun during These Days

Ogun has many qualities, such as strength and bravery, a strong sense of justice, as well as benevolence, and healing. Consider visiting a local temple or shrine dedicated to Ogun and sharing your offerings of candles or alcohol. You can also take time to reflect on the symbolization of Ogun, with offerings of black and red cloth to represent its colors in syncretism. Remember that if you are observing the day for the first time, it's okay for your devotion not to be perfect, but it can still be a meaningful ritual, nonetheless.

Here are some more tips for celebrating Ogun's festival, whether you are alone or with friends:

- Spend time meditating and reflecting on the qualities of Ogun and why they are important.
- Create a personal altar to show your devotion - gather items that symbolize Ogun's strength and fortitude.
- Spend some time journaling - write down your gratitude for Ogun's protection or any challenges you have faced over the past year and how his presence has helped you overcome them.
- Hold a ceremony with friends or family to honor Ogun: dress in red and black, light candles, and read prayers or poems dedicated to the Orisha.

- Share stories of Ogun's many feats or of how his presence has impacted your life.
- Finally, enjoy a traditional Nigerian feast to honor the Orisha – you can make this meal yourself or order delivery from a local Nigerian restaurant.

Ogun's festival is an incredible event that celebrates the strength and resilience of its namesake. By taking part in the festivities, you can connect with him and receive his protection during your journey. Through thoughtful reflection, meaningful ceremonies, and delicious meals, you can honor the Orisha and continue to remain determined in pursuit of your goals. So, gather your friends or find a quiet spot to reflect; it's time to celebrate Ogun!

Chapter 10: Daily Rituals to Celebrate Ogun

Ogun, the African Orisha of Iron, is a deity with a passionate spirit who can bring a blessing or curse upon people. Aligning with this singular warrior's energy daily is incredibly rewarding for those brave enough to do so. This can be accomplished through offering prayers, performing rituals, and engaging in activities that acknowledge and honor his empowering presence. Those who align with Ogun's strength experience great protection, stamina, and resourcefulness while they walk their life paths.

For those looking for a deeper connection to Ogun, take the time to honor him daily and watches your life transform. This chapter explains how to venerate him and align with Ogun's energy daily. It provides ideas and rituals, prayers, spiritual baths, and activities one can do each day of the week. Each activity holds a blessing, from protection against negative thought patterns to working towards a goal or deepening your connection to the divine. By engaging in each of these daily activities, you'll move closer to Ogun and experience a deeper connection with him.

Prayers to Ogun

Invoking Ogun through prayer is a powerful way to honor the Yoruba deity of metallurgy and physical power. Ogun is known and respected across many African cultures, including Nigeria and Benin. In Yoruba tradition, special rituals and prayers to Ogun have been practiced for centuries. Often these include burning cigars or incense, which is said to help communicate with the spirit world. To receive the blessings of Ogun, it is essential to pay respect and reverence by engaging in sacred prayers. Worshippers may find their spirits filled with power and strength when they connect with Ogun through prayer.

Rituals for Aligning with Ogun

Taking part in rituals that call upon Ogun can be a powerful and meaningful way to align oneself with his spirit. Often, these rituals involve offering prayers and songs while garbed in colors such as red, white, or black. Other offerings for Ogun might include tools such as axes and hammers, money, or other metal items that symbolically represent strength or fortitude. During the ritual, take some moments to set intentions of what you hope to gain by uniting with this mighty Orisha. Connecting with Ogun often leads to more clarity of purpose and brings strong spiritual and physical protection. Whether you are exploring a self-directed ritual ceremony or joining an established one, be sure to keep your eyes open and all your senses alert. You never know when help from Spirit will show up along the way!

Daily Activities That Honor Ogun

Every day, you can take part in activities that honor Ogun. From offering special drinks to the mischievous and powerful deity to telling stories of his strength, you can do your part in venerating him. Every morning pay homage to Ogun with a prayer. Every night, leave offerings out for the Orishas. Additionally, for more permanent gestures of appreciation and respect, people may create physical shrines or alter rooms in their homes solely dedicated to this popular god. Regardless of how you choose to honor him daily, you should remember that by participating in these activities, you are paying tribute to the creativity and power of Ogun.

Monday

The start of a new week can bring both excitement and anxiety. On Mondays, take the time to honor Ogun with the following rituals and activities.

1. Ritual: Protection against Negative Thought Patterns

Mondays can be rough, and it's easy to think negatively about what is traditionally the first day of the work week. By honoring Ogun, the god of power and strength, you can use rituals as protection against those negative cycles and have a great start to start. To begin, gather a few tools or items that represent Ogun's strength and power: such as an axe, hammer, knife, or other metal tools. Anoint yourself with oils dedicated to Ogun, such as frankincense or myrrh. Light a candle and say a prayer or mantra.

2. Activity: Learning a Craft

Mondays can become the start of a new beginning. Why not use it to learn something new? This is a great way to honor Ogun, the Yoruba spirit of iron and war. An activity such as candle- or soap-making works with Ogun's element of fire, and learning how to fabricate metal tools can be very fulfilling. Learning a craft also encourages strength of mind, body, and soul, which is needed to face life's challenges. It teaches you that hard work will lead to joy in the end.

3. Meditation: Connecting to Nature

Start your Monday with activities that bring clarity and focus to your mind, body, and spirit, such as taking a walk outdoors, doing deep breathing exercises, or writing in a gratitude journal. If you're creative, you could even make a physical representation of Ogun on the day. Draw or craft something that speaks to his power and place it where you'll see it often.

Tuesday

Fear and doubt can often creep up towards the middle of the week. Tuesday is a day to shed your worries and doubts, so you can keep marching forward confidently. On Tuesdays, use the following activities to align with Ogun and his energy:

1. Ritual: Protect Your Home from Unwanted Influences

Since Tuesdays are the day that honors Ogun, it is the perfect time to perform a ritual for protection. Begin by purifying your home and yourself with smoke from herbs such as sage or frankincense. Call upon Ogun to protect your home from any unwanted energies, negative entities, or evil influences. Gather metal tools and items that represent his strength, such as hammers, axes, knives, and swords. Place them all around your home to symbolize Ogun's protection.

2. Activity: Working with Metal Tools

On Tuesdays, it is especially fitting to do something that involves metal tools since this is Ogun's element. Try your hand at making tools out of metal, or find a class where you can learn to work with metal tools. Working with these materials will help you form a connection with Ogun and his power.

3. Meditation: Overcoming Fear

Take some time out of your day to meditate on overcoming fear. Fear can paralyze us and make it hard to move forward. By calling upon Ogun's power and strength, we can invoke the courage to overcome fear and make progress. Visualize yourself surrounded by a circle of metal tools, representing Ogun's protection. As you take deep breaths, imagine the fear dissipating and being replaced by steely courage and strength.

Wednesday

Negativity can be hard to shake, but on Wednesdays, you can use the following ideas to align with Ogun and his energy.

1. Ritual: Protection against Negative Thought Patterns

Wednesdays can be especially draining, and protecting yourself from negative energy is crucial. Begin the ritual by gathering items representative of Ogun's strength and power, such as an axe, hammer, knife, or other metal tools. Anoint yourself with the oils dedicated to Ogun. Visualize a bright white light surrounding you and say a prayer or mantra for protection.

2. Activity: Inventing Something New

Wednesdays are perfect for honoring Ogun by challenging yourself and pushing your creative boundaries. Spend some time inventing something new, whether it be a recipe, craft, or tool. Ogun is the spirit of creation and innovation. Celebrate his energy by coming up with something unique.

3. Meditation: Purification

Meditate on purifying your thoughts and emotions. During this meditation, visualize yourself surrounded by a bright white light of protection. Imagine the light entering your mind and body, purifying, and pushing out all negative thoughts, emotions, and energies. Call upon Ogun to help you stay focused on positive thoughts and maintain your strength against any negativity that may come your way.

Thursday

Cleansing and purifying are essential steps to take on Thursdays. Use the following ideas to honor Ogun and bring his energy into your life.

1. Ritual: Clearing Out Old Energy

Thursdays are a great day to honor Ogun and clear out any old energy that may be weighing you down. Begin by cleansing your home and yourself with smoke from herbs such as sage or frankincense. Then, take a spiritual bath to further purify your energy. As you bathe, call upon Ogun to help you clear out any old patterns and make room for new beginnings.

2. Activity: Taking a Spiritual Bath

You can use herbs such as lavender, rosemary, or eucalyptus to cleanse your aura of any stagnant energy. Begin the day by taking an herbal cleansing bath to purify your body and spirit. You can also create an herbal smudging stick using sage or lavender. As you do this, call upon Ogun for strength and protection.

3. Meditation: Letting Go of Attachments

Take some time to meditate on releasing any attachments that may be holding you back. It can be difficult to move forward when we cling too tightly to things or people. Visualize yourself surrounded by a circle of metal tools, representing Ogun's strength and guidance. As you take deep breaths, imagine the attachments being cut loose and fading away. Repeat a mantra such as "I let go of all that no longer serves me, in strength and courage."

Friday

Friday is the day to take the time to focus on your goals and ambitions. Here are some rituals and activities you can do to align yourself with Ogun

1. Ritual: Connecting to Your Path

Fridays are for focusing on connecting to your spiritual path. Start by lighting a white candle and calling upon Ogun for protection and guidance. Then, take a few moments to reflect on the goals you have set for yourself and how you can use Ogun's strength and courage to help you reach them.

2. Activity: Working towards a Goal

Take some time to focus on working towards a goal that you have set for yourself. Ogun is the spirit of progress, so use this day to tap into his energy and make strides toward achieving your goals. Whether it means taking classes, doing research, or reaching out for resources, take action to keep moving forward.

3. Meditation: Facing Difficult Tasks

Meditate and visualize yourself surrounded by Ogun's strength and protection in the face of difficult tasks. Call on Ogun's courage and strength to keep you motivated to get through the toughest of times. Focusing your energy in a positive direction will help you overcome any challenge that lies in your way.

Saturday

Being creative and inventive is key on Saturdays. Here are some rituals and activities you can do to align yourself with Ogun.

1. Ritual: Rituals to Unblock Creativity

Saturdays are a great day to focus on unblocking any creative energy that may be stuck. Begin by lighting a green candle and calling upon Ogun for creative inspiration. Then, spend some time engaging in rituals such as writing a poem or painting to help you reconnect with your inner artist.

2. Activity: Exploring the Unknown

Ogun is a spirit of exploration, so use this day to explore the unknown. Take time to wander through nature and see what new adventures present themselves. Get out of your comfort zone and try something new, such as a new craft or skill.

3. Meditation: Honoring Ancestors

Take some time to honor your ancestors and call upon Ogun to guide you on your journey. Imagine yourself surrounded by a circle of metal tools, representing the strength and protection of your ancestors. Close your eyes and reflect on the stories, wisdom, and knowledge that have been passed down to you from your ancestors.

Sunday

Hope and faith are the themes of Sundays. Here are some rituals and activities you can do to align yourself with Ogun

1. Ritual: Abundance and Opportunity

Sundays are a great day to focus on creating abundance and opportunity. Begin by lighting a yellow candle and calling upon Ogun to open the doors of abundance. Take some time to focus on manifesting the life that you want and creating a plan for achieving your goals.

2. Activity: Visiting a Shrine or Sanctuary

A great way to honor Ogun is to visit a shrine or sanctuary dedicated to him. Connect with his energy and offer prayers and gifts. You can also create your shrine in your home to keep Ogun's spirit close by.

3. Meditation: Deepening Your Connection

Take some time to meditate and deepen your connection with Ogun. Imagine yourself surrounded by a circle of metal tools, representing his strength and guidance. Visualize yourself embracing his energy and using it to empower you in your daily life.

These are just some ideas that can help you align with Ogun's energy on a day-to-day basis. Feel free to get creative and explore other rituals, activities, and meditations to help you connect to him more deeply. Remember, Ogun is the spirit of progress and transformation, so use his energy as your guide on your journey.

Extra: Glossary of Terms

This extra chapter provides a comprehensive glossary of terms to help you navigate the book more easily. Below, you'll find an alphabetical list of foreign words and their definitions, accompanied by pronunciation and phonetics.

Baron Samedi (bah-RAWN sah-MEH-dee): Baron Samedi is a deity of the dead in Haitian Vodou.

Damballah (dahm-buh-LAH): The great serpent spirit of the heavens, also known as a "great sky father."

Obatala (oh-bah-TAH-lah): The Orisha of peace, justice

Ifa (ee-fah): A spiritual or divinatory system that is the foundation of Yoruba religion.

Loa (low-ah): A spirit in Haitian Vodou.

Obatala (oh-bah-tuh-lah): The Orisha of creation, peace, and purity. Obatala loves harmony and justice in all things.

Ogun (Oh-goon): The Orisha of iron, war, and labor. He is known to resolve difficult situations and protect or defend his devotees.

Oggun Akomi (Oh-goon ah-KOH-mee): One of the seven paths of Ogun, also known as the path of healing and creativity.

Oggun Alagbo (Oh-goon ah-lah-GOH-bo): One of the seven paths of Ogun, also known as the path of wisdom and knowledge.

Oggun Irumole (Oh-goon eer-oo-MOH-lee): One of the seven paths of Ogun, also known as the path of spiritual awakening.

Oggun Meji (Oh-goon meh-jee): One of the seven paths of Ogun, also known as the path of communication and strength.

Oggun Onile (Oh-goon oh-NEE-lee): One of the seven paths of Ogun, also known as the path of movement and traveling.

Oggun Oloyon (Oh-goon oh-low-YOHN): One of the seven paths of Ogun, also known as the path of helping others.

Oggun Oyeku Meji (Oh-goon oh-yay-koo meh-jee): One of the seven paths of Ogun, also known as the path of courage.

Orisa (or-ee-sah): Deities or divine beings in the Yoruba pantheon, venerated in both Africa and the African diaspora.

Yemeya (yay-may-yah): The Orisha of the sea, ruler over storms and shipwrecks. She is often invoked to protect sailors and travelers.

Yoruba (Yoh-roo-bah): The language spoken by the Yoruba people of Nigeria in West Africa.

Conclusion

Ogun is a fascinating deity who forms an important part of the belief system of the Yoruba people. He had a long and complicated history for hundreds of years before becoming firmly entrenched in Yoruba mythology and culture as the god of ironwork and war. Ogun is called on by his followers to remove obstacles, allowing them to overcome challenges and create their own destinies. Today, he is still worshipped by many adherents of traditional Yoruba beliefs throughout Nigeria.

Ogun, the god of knowledge, power, and creativity, is a source of great strength and guidance. His continuous presence is comforting to those looking for help in times of need. While Ogun is primarily associated with ironwork and war, he also has strong connections to protection, justice, trustworthiness, and the spirit of progress. He is also considered to be both a saint and a warrior.

Whether it is his powerful grace that protects us from harm or his creative genius that helps us find solutions when all else fails, Ogun finds a way to give meaning to life and restore balance in the universe. He knows no boundaries and will always be there for you, no matter the situation. To seek counsel from Ogun is to tap into an infinite source of wisdom and protection, delivering clarity in times of distress.

Ogun has been a legendary figure for centuries. He is credited for having inspired many aspects of the Yoruba people's vibrant culture. For example, he has been invoked in various literary and artistic works as a symbol of strength. He also is given immense respect due to his representation of life-sustaining powers like creativity and productivity.

His influence extends to different realms, such as spiritual, political, economic, and social. It continues to shape how the Yoruba people identify and live today. Regardless of their specific faith, it is impossible to deny Ogun's monumental effects on Yoruba cultural identity throughout history.

This guide provided a comprehensive overview of Ogun, focusing on the history and mythology surrounding his cultic following, how to identify as a child of Ogun, and the rituals, symbols, and festivals associated with him. It also includes information on setting up a sacred altar, performing useful rituals and spells, and celebrating Ogun through daily practices. Finally, a glossary of relevant terms and phrases is included for easy reference.

Through this guide, we hope you gained a deeper understanding of Ogun and will come to appreciate his power and presence in your life. By following his teachings, you can make significant progress on the path of life and achieve your goals. Ogun is always with you, helping you to create a brighter future.

Here's another book by Mari Silva that you might like

Your Free Gift
(only available for a limited time)

Thanks for getting this book! If you want to learn more about various spirituality topics, then join Mari Silva's community and get a free guided meditation MP3 for awakening your third eye. This guided meditation mp3 is designed to open and strengthen ones third eye so you can experience a higher state of consciousness. Simply visit the link below the image to get started.

https://spiritualityspot.com/meditation

References

Nigeria, G. (2019, November 24). The Orisha Ogun in Maleficent. The Guardian Nigeria News - Nigeria and World News; Guardian Nigeria. https://guardian.ng/life/the-orisha-ogun-in-maleficent/

Ogun. (n.d.-a). Encyclopedia.com. https://www.encyclopedia.com/humanities/news-wires-white-papers-and-books/ogun

Ogun. (n.d.-b). Mythencyclopedia.com. http://www.mythencyclopedia.com/Ni-Pa/Ogun.html

Ogun, god of war. (n.d.). Africanpoems.net. https://africanpoems.net/gods-ancestors/ogun-god-of-war/

Olive senior's gardening in the tropics. (n.d.). Torontomu.Ca. https://www.torontomu.ca/olivesenior/poems/ogun.html

Origin of Ogun – god of iron. (2016, December 30). Ondo Connects New Era. http://www.ekimogundescendant.org/origin-of-ogun-god-of-iron/

XoticBrands. (2020, December 4). Ogun, God of Iron and Rum…Who was he in 3 mins? Medium. https://xoticbrands.medium.com/ogun-god-of-iron-and-rum-4e68172f9af7

www.ingramcontent.com/pod-product-compliance
Lightning Source LLC
Chambersburg PA
CBHW072153200426
43209CB00052B/1166